not just desserts

sweet herbal recipes

susan belsinger

SO-CFL-844

copyright page

not just desserts sweet herbal recipes
susan belsinger ©

photography, susan belsinger
cover design, jeff st.clair
author photo, nanette hatzes
editing, pat crocker and carolyn dille
publisher, herbspirit
living with herbs series

text copyright 2005, susan belsinger
photography copyright 2005, susan belsinger

first printing:
paul's printing
po box 147
reeds spring, mo 65737

second printing:
creative printing & design
139 industrial park drive
hollister, mo 65672

isbn # 0-9766771-0-5

dedication

for tina marie
dear friend and herbal cohort
whose knowledge and love of herbs
is an inspiration
may these recipes whet
your near insatiable sweet tooth.

acknowledgements

this book is a collection of recipes from articles, books, and handouts that i have developed and written over the past 20 years or so. i have been inspired and enthusiastically supported by gardeners and cooks across the nation—both novices and pros—and i thank each and every one of you.

i especially want to thank carolyn dille, who began this journey with me many years ago—some of our first recipes are still here—for her nurturing and sustaining friendship. and to pat crocker for sharing our mutual writing and editing skills back and forth.

i must also acknowledge *herb companion* and *natural home and garden magazine* for letting me share my recently printed recipes from 2004-2005.

without the love and sustenance of my family, i could never have followed my garden path into the kitchen and been able to create, write, and teach about these things that i love to do. this support spans the elder generations—from my grandmothers who passed on their family recipes that we grew up eating—to my parents, audrey and bobbo, who helped shape who i am today.

my deep gratitude to tomaso for being the consummate handyman, whether it is to fix yet another computer problem, rototill or weed, hold down the fort, or taste yet another recipe test. and to the now generation—my beautiful daughters, lucie and cady—thank you for being just who you are. i appreciate the years of trying just one bite, and learning to give me feedback to my probing questions as to how things taste and smell. i am grateful for your helping in the garden and the kitchen, and for learning to like the green specks in your food. hopefully, these experiences will help nourish you throughout your lives, and that you will pass on the love of green growing things and good food to your children, the future generation.

contents

introduction

Although this book contains mostly recipes for desserts, I decided to call it **not just desserts** because the recipes are much more than that. This compilation of recipes has evolved from over 25 years of gardening and cooking, writing books, articles, and handouts, teaching classes, and giving lectures and demonstrations. However, the single most important ingredient to this collection of recipes are herbs.

I have been gardening and cooking my way through a life filled with herbs for about 30 years now. They are essential to my kitchen and they sweeten each day with their fragrance and flavor. I use herbs in all parts of a meal—from soups and savories to salads and baked goods—**not just desserts.** Using herbs to flavor any food, whether sweet or savory, will elevate it to another level. Herbs can complement, accentuate, intensify, echo, and insinuate themselves on a dish. They can take over and command a dish as basil does *pesto*, or they can give just a hint of flavor as a bay leaf lifts a *béchamel.* Bold or subtle, herbs can make a ho-hum recipe outstanding.

The **sweet herbal recipes** herein are simple, homey desserts. Some of them are traditional recipes, variations on a theme, or an old family favorite, while some are new and innovative, or perhaps to some, downright peculiar. All of them are made delicious because of the addition of herbs.

Over the years of working with herbs, I have come to know them well, and they are quite individual in their character. You might say that I have an intimate relationship with them.

Through sensory experience, I am stimulated by them daily. My eyes are delighted by their new growth, leaf shapes, and many hues, not to mention the dancing colors of their blooms. My hands reach out to stroke the velvet texture of a sage leaf or to gently squeeze the resinous needles of rosemary. I hear the buzz of bees as they busily go about their task of pollination, spending long lazy days in the lavender bed, or the wind rustling the seed pods of sesame.

My nose is probably the sense most influenced, as I am regularly seduced by the many scents of herbs. Who is not stopped dead in their tracks through the garden when the spring breeze ruffles the lilacs and fills the air with that heady perfume, or when that first summer *Rosa rugosa* opens? The fragrance of herbs is the foreplay of flavor. Without smell, we could not taste. When we smell mint, our olfactory sense processes the information so fast, we hardly realize that we are being inundated with smell and taste memories from everything relating to mint in our lives from toothpaste and chewing gum to our grandmother's bowl of peppermints or a cup of mint tea. We smell those chocolate mint brownies baking and begin salivating long before we take a bite.

Suffice all of this to say, that herbs add another dimension to our lives, especially in the kitchen. Hopefully these **sweet herbal recipes** will inspire you to experiment with and add more herbs to your cooking. Think of this as one big sweet herbal adventure.

If you don't have anise hyssop, use another herb that you might like the flavor of and substitute it. If a recipe calls for lemon balm, you can replace it with a different lemon-flavored herb such as lemon verbena, lemon grass, lemon thyme, or lemon basil.

When experimenting with herbs in a recipe, remember to pause for a minute, think about the aroma and taste of the herb or herbs, and how it will work with the other ingredients in the recipe. The whole idea of this book is to be creative, experiment, and use herbs to give new flavor and fun to your desserts.

There are all of the typical chapters here that you would see in any dessert cookbook. The ingredients used are familiar flavors like chocolate, vanilla, and seasonal fruit. I've listed herbs that partner well with chocolate in the chocolate chapter, herbs that complement fruit in the fruit chapter, and herbs that are good in syrups and scented sugars in the miscellaneous chapter.

When I cook, I take into consideration combining flavors, as well as using foods that are in season together. For example, using a fresh, spring strawberry with a strong, robust winter herb like sage would probably not result in a winning flavor combination. However, if you take that strawberry and combine it with an herbal harbinger of spring like sweet woodruff, mint, or lemon balm, you will have a harmonious joining of flavor. Any of these spring herbs will create a delightful, bright taste with the strawberry.

On the other hand, if you pair fall fruits such as apples or pears with the earthy musk of sage, you can make a tasty tart, applesauce, or fruit butter. It is the herbs in combination with good-quality ingredients that makes these recipes something out-of-the-ordinary—it lifts them up and really makes them sing!

I hope that once you have used this book and tried your hand with some of the recipes that you will agree with me that these are **not just desserts.**

strawberry rhubarb cobbler with sweet woodruff

herbal butter cookies and milk

cookies & bars

herbal butter cookies

three-seed cookies with citrus-flavored herbs

chewy chocolate cookies with rosemary,
pine nuts, & dried cherries

chocolate chip peanut butter oatmeal cookies

chocolate butter cookies with anise hyssop

chocolate chip roasted garlic cookies
& ice cream sandwiches

blondies with monarda & apricots

cranberry nut bars with rosemary

fudgey mint brownies with cocoa & mint
whipped cream

herbal butter cookies

Delightful with tea, or a glass of red wine, these cookies are simple to make and any herb can be used, however my favorites are any variety of rosemary, 'Aussie Sweetie' basil (cinnamon and spice flavored), and orange mint. You can use any of the mints or lemon herbs here. They keep well in a tin, or up to 2 months in the freezer.

Makes about 3 to 4 dozen cookies

> **12 tablespoons unsalted butter, softened**
> **2/3 cup sugar**
> **1 large egg**
> **1/2 teaspoon vanilla extract**
> **2 cups unbleached white flour, sifted**
> **2 to 3 tablespoons minced fresh herb leaves**
> **Pinch of salt**

Cream the butter and sugar. Beat in the egg and the extract. Gradually mix in the flour, and stir in the minced herb and a pinch of salt. The dough will be soft. Divide the dough into 2 parts. Using plastic wrap to shape the dough, roll each part into a cylinder about 1-1/4-inches in diameter. Chill the rolls for an hour, or place in the freezer for 20 minutes.

Preheat the oven to 350°F. Remove the plastic wrap and slice the dough into 1/4-inch rounds. Place the cookies on ungreased baking sheets and bake for about 10 minutes, until the cookies are a light golden brown. Remove the cookies from the baking sheets while they are hot and cool on racks.

chewy chocolate cookies with rosemary, pine nuts & dried cherries

three-seed cookies with citrus-flavored herbs

I first created this recipe using orange mint and orange zest. However it also works really well with lemon balm or lemon verbena and lemon zest. These good-for-you cookies are full of flavor; the recipe can easily be halved. I make a big batch and freeze some to have on hand. My kids refer to these as birdseed cookies.

Makes about 7 dozen cookies

3 sticks unsalted butter (1-1/2 cups), softened
1 cup light brown sugar
1 cup sugar
4 large eggs
1/2 teaspoon orange or lemon oil, optional
1 teaspoon pure vanilla extract
2 teaspoons orange or lemon zest
1/2 cup packed orange mint or lemon balm leaves, or
1/3 cup lemon verbena leaves, minced fine
2 cups unbleached flour
1 cup white whole wheat or whole wheat pastry flour
3/4 teaspoon salt
1-1/2 teaspoons baking soda
1/2 cup rolled oats
1/4 cup poppy seed
1/4 cup sesame seed
1/4 cup flax seed

Preheat oven to 350ºF and lightly butter two baking sheets.

In a large bowl, food processor, or mixer, beat the butter with the white and brown sugars until blended and fluffy. Beat in the eggs one at a time. Add the citrus oil, vanilla, zest, and herbs and blend well.

In a mixing bowl, combine the flours, salt, baking soda, oats, and seeds. Add the dry ingredients all at once to the wet and blend well.

Drop the dough by rounded teaspoonful onto baking sheets at least 2-inches apart. Bake until golden brown on the edges for about 10 to 12 minutes. Remove from baking sheets and cool on baking racks. Store in a tightly covered container.

chewy chocolate cookies with rosemary, pine nuts, and dried cherries

These unusual cookies, rich in chocolate, have resinous over-tones of rosemary, echoed by the pine and nutty flavors of pine nuts, and subtlety teased by the tart/sour/sweet of the dried cherries. The basic chocolate cookie recipe (without the herbs, nuts, and fruits) was inspired by the 911 Chocolate Emergency Cookies in Diane Mott Davidson's *Dying for Chocolate*. I especially like this combination at holiday time and they freeze well.

Makes about 5 dozen 2-1/2-inch cookies

- 12 ounces semisweet, bittersweet, or a combination of good quality chocolate
- 4 tablespoons unsalted butter
- 2-1/2 cups unbleached white flour
- 2/3 cup unsweetened cocoa
- 2 teaspoons baking powder
- 3/4 teaspoons salt
- 8 tablespoons unsalted butter, softened
- 1-1/4 cups packed dark brown sugar
- 3/4 cup granulated sugar
- 4 extra-large eggs
- 2 teaspoons pure vanilla extract
- 2 generous tablespoons fresh minced rosemary
- 3/4 cup pine nuts
- 1 cup coarsely chopped dried cherries

Preheat oven to 350°F and butter 2 baking sheets.

Break the chocolate into pieces. In a double boiler or the microwave, melt the chocolate with 4 tablespoons of butter, stir, and set aside.

Sift the flour, cocoa, baking powder, and salt into a separate bowl.

In a large bowl, beat 8 tablespoons softened butter with the brown and white sugars. Continue beating and add the eggs, one at a time. Add the vanilla and melted chocolate and mix until combined. Stir in the flour mixture, rosemary, pine nuts, and dried cherries and mix until blended.

The dough can be covered and refrigerated at this point for up to a few hours, or the cookies can be baked immediately. Drop the cookies by the heaping teaspoon onto the baking sheets about 2 inches apart. Bake in a hot oven for about 8 to 10 minutes, changing baking positions halfway through baking. The cookies should puff a little and flatten. Do not over bake them—they will firm up as they cool. Cool on baking sheets for a few minutes and then remove onto racks to cool. Store in airtight containers for a week or in the freezer for up to 3 months.

chocolate chip peanut butter oatmeal cookies

Three favorite cookies all rolled into one—these delectable treats are full of protein—and appeal to the kid in all of us. Although these cookies don't really have any green herbs in them—they do have chocolate in them (which I consider to be an essential herb)—so I included them because they are one of my favorites.

Makes about 4 dozen cookies

16 tablespoons unsalted butter (2 sticks), softened
3/4 cup peanut butter
1 cup demerara, turbinado, or regular sugar
1/2 cup dark brown sugar
2 extra-large eggs
2 teaspoons pure vanilla extract
1-1/2 cups unbleached flour
1/2 cup whole-wheat flour
1-1/4 teaspoons baking powder
3/4 teaspoon salt
1-1/2 cups oats
1 to 1-1/2 cups chocolate chips

Preheat oven to 350°F.

In a food processor or a large mixing bowl, combine the butter and peanut butter and process or beat with a wooden spoon until well blended. Add the sugars and process or stir until combined. Beat in the eggs, one at a time, and add the vanilla, blend well until smooth and creamy.

18

In a small bowl, combine the flour, whole-wheat flour, baking powder, and salt. Add the dry ingredients to the wet, and process, stopping to scrape down the sides, or mix well with a wooden spoon. The dough will be stiff.

Stir in the oats and chocolate chips. Drop the dough by the rounded tablespoonful about 2-inches apart on ungreased baking sheets. Flatten the dough with your fingers, or a fork if desired.

Bake the cookies in a preheated oven for 10 to 12 minutes, until they are just golden brown. Remove to baking racks to cool. They will keep, stored in a tightly closed tin or plastic container for a week, or they can be frozen for up to a month.

chocolate butter cookies with anise hyssop

You can use both the leaves and the flowers of anise hyssop, but the flowers have a higher oil content, thus a stronger taste. You could also use tarragon or fennel for a similar anise flavor. Mint or lavender is also good in place of the anise-flavored herbs in this cookie recipe. They keep well in a tin or up to 2 months in the freezer.

Makes about 5 dozen cookies

> **1/3 cup anise hyssop flowers and bracts, or leaves**
> **1 cup sugar**
> **1 extra-large egg**
> **12 tablespoons unsalted butter, softened**
> **2 ounces unsweetened chocolate, melted**
> **2 cups unbleached white flour**
> **1/2 teaspoon salt**

Combine the hyssop and sugar in the food processor and pulse until blended. Add the butter and pulse. Beat in the egg and the chocolate. Gradually mix in the flour and salt.

The dough will be soft. Divide the dough into 2 parts. Using plastic wrap to shape the dough, roll each part into a cylinder about 1-1/2-inches in diameter. Chill the rolls for an hour, or place in the freezer for 20 to 30 minutes.

Preheat the oven to 350°F. Remove the plastic wrap and slice the dough into 1/4-inch rounds. Place the cookies on ungreased baking sheets and bake for about 10 minutes, until the cookies are light brown. Remove the cookies from the baking sheets while they are hot and cool on racks.

chocolate chip roasted garlic cookies & ice cream sandwiches

When garlic is roasted it turns nutty sweet and loses its pungency. For this recipe the garlic is roasted in nut oil which emphasizes the nuttiness—I like walnut and hazelnut oil best—you could use peanut or almond oil, but they don't really have a nutty flavor. I generally use the same type of nut in the cookies as the oil that I roast the garlic in (i.e.: walnuts or pecans with walnut oil, hazelnuts with hazelnut oil, macadamia nuts with macadamia oil, etc.) Don't tell your guests what the secret ingredient is and make them guess—even with a hint that it is an herb—they never do!

Makes about 4 dozen 2-inch cookies or 2-1/2 dozen 3-inch cookies

- **1 bulb garlic**
- **1/4 cup nut oil**
- **12 tablespoons unsalted butter (1-1/2 sticks), softened**
- **1 cup sugar**
- **1/2 cup dark brown sugar**
- **2 extra-large eggs**
- **2 teaspoons pure vanilla extract**
- **1-1/2 cups unbleached flour**
- **1/2 cup whole-wheat flour**
- **Scant cup of rolled oats**
- **1-1/4 teaspoons baking powder**
- **3/4 teaspoon salt**
- **1-1/2 cups chocolate chips**
- **1 cup coarsely chopped nuts**

Preheat oven to 325°F. Remove the outer papery skins of the garlic and break the garlic bulb into cloves; leave the inner skins on the cloves. Place the garlic in a small oven-proof dish and add the nut oil. Cover the dish with foil. Bake the garlic until it is very tender; check it in about 30 to 35 minutes. It will take about 45 minutes to roast this many cloves. Test for doneness by squeezing a clove or two—it should be soft and golden. Remove from the oven and let the garlic cool a bit. When it is cool enough to handle, squeeze the cloves of roasted garlic into the oil and discard the skins.

In a food processor or a mixing bowl, combine the butter, roasted garlic, and the nut oil and process, or mash the garlic with a fork and beat ingredients together with a wooden spoon until well blended. Add the sugars and process or stir until combined. Beat in the eggs and add the vanilla, blend well until smooth and creamy.

In a small bowl, combine the flour, whole-wheat flour, oats, baking powder, and salt. Add the dry ingredients to the wet, and process, stopping to scrape down the sides, or mix well with a wooden spoon. The dough will be stiff.

Stir in the chocolate chips and nuts. Drop the dough by the rounded tablespoonful about 2-inches apart on ungreased baking sheets. For ice cream sandwiches, I drop the cookies by a generous heaping tablespoonful to make a bigger cookie. Moisten your fingers with cold water and press the cookie dough flat, or use a fork if desired.

Bake the cookies in a preheated 350°F oven for 10 to 12 minutes, until they are just golden brown. Remove to baking racks to cool. They will keep, stored in a tightly closed tin or plastic container for a week, or they can be frozen for up to a month.

ice cream sandwiches

1 batch of prepared cookies
1/2 gallon good-quality vanilla ice cream

To assemble ice cream sandwiches, set the ice cream out at room temperature for about 10 minutes to soften slightly. Using an ice cream scoop, scoop a rounded scoop onto the bottom of one cookie and place another cookie, bottom-side toward the ice cream, on top. Press the cookies gently to squeeze the ice cream so that it reaches to the outer edges of the cookies.

Place the ice cream sandwiches onto a baking sheet in a single layer and freeze until hard. At this point you can individually wrap the ice cream sandwiches in plastic, or you can place them in a tightly sealed container and freeze until ready to eat. They should be made a few hours in advance so they have a chance to set up and become hardened. They will keep for a few days if well-wrapped. This recipe will make about 12 to 15 ice cream sandwiches.

blondies with monarda & apricots (or bergamot bars)

For the best flavor, these bars should be made with butter for a good butterscotch taste. Use the red-flowered *Monarda didyma* (also known as beebalm and bergamot) since the other monardas have an oregano-like flavor and would not be good in a dessert. Orange mint can be substituted for the monarda.

9 x 13-inch pan; makes 32 bars

1 cup (2 sticks) unsalted butter
1 1/3 cups packed, light brown sugar
2/3 cup granulated sugar
About 1 cup dried apricots
About 1/2 cup monarda leaves, loosely packed
2-1/2 cups unbleached flour
2 teaspoons baking powder
1 teaspoon salt
3 extra-large eggs
1-1/2 teaspoons pure vanilla extract

Preheat oven to 350°F. Butter a 13 x 9 x 2-inch pan.

In a heavy-bottomed, medium saucepan, melt the butter over medium-low heat. When melted, add the brown sugar and stir. Cook over medium-low heat, stirring, until the brown sugar is thick and syrupy, for about 4 minutes. Stir in the granulated sugar until it is dissolved and remove the pan from the heat to cool.

Thinly slice the apricots crosswise. Wash, dry, and coarsely chop the monarda leaves, there should be about 3 tablespoons of chopped herb.

Combine the flour, baking powder, and salt in a bowl and stir to blend. Sprinkle 1 tablespoon of the flour mixture over the apricots and toss to coat them lightly.

Beat the eggs into the warm brown sugar and butter mixture (it should not be hot) to blend thoroughly. Add the vanilla and stir well.

Pour the liquid ingredients into the flour and stir until it is just blended. Add the apricots and monarda and stir until they are just mixed in. Pour the batter into the prepared pan and bake in a preheated oven for 35 minutes, until the top is a deep golden brown. Allow to cool completely on a baking rack before cutting into bars.

cranberry nut bars with rosemary

These buttery bars are full of flavor—tart with dried fruit, sweet with brown sugar, chock full of nuts—and fragrant with a pleasant surprise of rosemary. Use the larger amount of rosemary for a stronger herbal flavor, or the smaller quantity for a milder taste. I like these best when made with hazelnuts that have been toasted and rubbed from their skins, but pecans and walnuts are equally good.

9 x 13-inch pan; makes 24 to 32 bars

- 10 tablespoons unsalted butter, cut into pieces
- 1 2/3 cups firmly packed light brown sugar
- 1-1/2 cups unbleached flour
- Pinch salt
- 3 extra-large eggs
- 1-1/2 teaspoons pure vanilla extract
- Zest of 1 orange
- 1/2 teaspoon salt
- 1-1/2 teaspoons baking powder
- 1 cup hazelnuts, chopped coarse or pecan or walnut halves
- Scant cup dried cranberries or dried cherries, roughly chopped
- 3 to 4 tablespoons fresh minced rosemary leaves

Preheat oven to 375°F and lightly butter a 9 x 13-inch pan. In a food processor or a bowl, combine the butter, 2/3 cup brown sugar, 1-1/4 cups of the flour, and pinch of salt. Pulse just until crumbly, or mix in a bowl with a pastry blender. Pat the crust into the prepared pan and bake for 12 to 14 minutes until just barely golden brown. Remove from oven and let cool a bit. Reduce oven temperature to 350°F.

In the food processor or a bowl, beat the eggs with the remaining cup of brown sugar and blend well. Add the vanilla, orange zest, remaining 1/4 cup of flour, 1/2 teaspoon of salt, and baking powder and blend well. Stir the rosemary into the batter. Evenly spread the nuts and cranberries over the crust. Pour the egg mixture over the nuts and cranberries on the crust.

Bake for 22 to 25 minutes, or until the center is baked and the bars are a deep golden brown. Cool the pan on a baking rack and them cut into bars.

For smaller bars, divide the pan into rows of 4 by 8 pieces, and for larger bars, cut them into 4 by 6 pieces. Store the bars in an airtight container.

fudgey mint brownies
with cocoa & mint whipped cream

Mint is an age-old combination with chocolate and although mint is generally thought of as a cooling herb, both spearmint and peppermint have long been considered as aphrodisiacs. Shakespeare recommended it as a stimulant for middle-aged gentlemen. The cocoa whipped cream is a decadent accompaniment, which elevates this dessert to more than the average brownie and it may inspire you to use it in other ways.

If you don't have fresh mint and must use dried—use about 3 tablespoons of leaves in the brownies, crushed, and 1 tablespoon in the cream, crushed (which you will have to strain). Dried mint will not impart the fresh aroma that fresh mint contains, so you might add a few drops of peppermint extract, but don't overdo it.

9 x 13-inch pan; makes about 24 brownies

8 ounces unsweetened chocolate
1 cup unsalted butter (2 sticks)
2-1/2 cups sugar
4 extra-large eggs
1-1/2 teaspoons pure vanilla extract
1/2 cup fresh mint leaves, minced fine
1-1/2 cups unbleached flour
1/2 teaspoon salt

Preheat the oven to 375°F. Butter a 13 x 9-inch baking pan and line it with foil. Generously butter and lightly flour the foil.

Combine the chocolate and butter, melt over low heat on the stovetop or in a microwave. Stir the sugar into the melted chocolate and butter. Beat the eggs into the mixture one at a time, and then add the vanilla and mint. Stir in the flour with the salt until just mixed. Pour and scrape the brownie mix into the prepared pan and smooth it out evenly in the pan.

Bake in a preheated oven for 30 to 35 minutes. The edges should be drawing away from the sides of the pan and a toothpick inserted about an inch from the edge should come out clean. If inserted in the center it will still be a little sticky, which results in a fudgier brownie, bake a little longer if you like them a little more crisp. Cool completely before removing the brownies from the pan by loosening the foil and lifting them out. Cut brownies with a sharp knife—they will be sticky—store them in a tightly-closed container.

cocoa whipped cream with mint

1 pint heavy whipping cream
4 or 5 mint sprigs
3 tablespoons unsweetened cocoa
3 tablespoons sugar

In a deep bowl, combine the whipping cream, mint, and cocoa. Bruise the mint leaves against the side of the bowl with a wooden spoon and stir to blend in cocoa. Cover and infuse in the refrigerator for one hour or up to overnight.

Remove the mint sprigs, squeezing them to remove excess liquid. Whisk the cream until it just starts to thicken and add the sugar. Whisk until soft peaks form. Serve a dollop on each brownie. This can be made in advance and kept in the fridge—if it gets a little thin—just whisk it up again.

chocolate pudding with bay

puddings, custards, & creams

lemon balm custard with rhubarb sauce

stovetop rice pudding with bay

decadent vanilla crème brulee

luscious lemon cream

chocolate pudding with bay

lemon balm custard
with rhubarb sauce

Lemon balm is a harbinger in our spring gardens. If you don't have lemon balm—you can use about a tablespoon of dried lemon verbena leaves or 2 fresh bay leaves—if you don't have these herbs, the lemon zest and vanilla give adequate flavor for this simple, classic custard. The tartness of the rhubarb sauce is a wonderful counterpoint to the smooth custard. The custard can be unmolded and served with a warm sauce, or they can be refrigerated and served at cool room temperature, with the sauce at room temperature or warmed. Both the custard and sauce can be prepared a day in advance. If you are too busy and don't have time to make the custard, this sauce is great on vanilla ice cream.

Makes six 6-ounce or eight 4-ounce ramekins or custard cups

custard

2-1/2 cups milk
1/2 cup fresh lemon balm or 2 bay fresh leaves
Generous teaspoon lemon zest
1/2 vanilla bean, split lengthwise or 1 teaspoon pure
vanilla extract
1/2 cup sugar
2 extra-large whole eggs
2 extra-large egg yolks
pinch salt

In a heavy-bottomed nonreactive pan, heat the milk with the herbs, lemon zest, and the vanilla bean if you are using it, and bring to a simmer. Remove from heat, cover, and let stand for about 1/2 hour.

Place 6 ramekins or custard cups in an ovenproof pan, which can hold them without touching.

Preheat oven to 325°F. Add the sugar to the milk-herb mixture and gently reheat over medium heat to dissolve the sugar, stirring occasionally. In a small bowl, lightly beat the eggs with the egg yolks and a pinch of salt. Pour or spoon about ? cup of the warm milk into the eggs and whisk to incorporate. Then add all of the milk to the eggs and blend well. Add vanilla extract, if not using the bean.

Pour the custard mixture through a strainer to remove the herbs, zest, and vanilla bean, pressing them gently to remove their essence. Pour the custard mix evenly into the custard dishes. Pour hot water into the pan to come halfway up the sides of the cups. Place the pan in the preheated oven and bake the custards until they are set, about 40 minutes, or until a knife inserted in the center comes out clean.

Remove the custards from the hot water and place on a baking rack to cool. Serve warm, or, cool and refrigerate. The custard may be served in the dish it was baked in, or unmolded by gently running a spatula around the edges of the dish and inverting it onto a serving plate.

rhubarb sauce

If you have lemon balm, or sweet woodruff, add a handful of the leaves to the rhubarb sauce along with the rest of the ingredients, and remove them before serving. This sauce makes a little more than needed, but will keep in the refrigerator for a week. It is delicious on ice cream, waffles, pancakes, biscuits, peach pie, and with yogurt or oatmeal.

4 cups finely chopped fresh rhubarb
1/2 cup orange juice, preferably fresh-squeezed
1/2 cup sugar
1 to 2-inch piece vanilla bean, split lengthwise
few dashes fresh grated nutmeg

Scrub the rhubarb, trim the ends, and cut lengthwise down the center. Cut the rhubarb into 1/4-inch slices.

Combine the rhubarb, orange juice, sugar, vanilla bean, nutmeg, and herbs if you are using them, in a large heavy-bottomed, nonreactive saucepan and place over medium high heat. Stir, cover and bring to a simmer, which will just take a few minutes. Remove lid, stir well, reduce heat to medium. Cover and cook for 5 minutes. Remove lid, stir, and turn off heat.

Cover and let stand, the sauce will continue to cook a little as it stands. The sauce should be about the consistency of a thick soup. If you want it thicker, cook it a few minutes more with the lid off. Remove the herbs and vanilla bean pieces before serving. Serve warm or at cool room temperature; it can be easily reheated.

stovetop rice pudding with bay

This is an ideal way to use leftover rice—either white or brown—if you cook your rice with salt, omit the salt in the recipe ingredients. It can be served warm right from the stove, at room temperature, or cold. If you refrigerate it, let it sit at room temperature for about 10 minutes before serving. Reheat gently on stovetop or in the microwave, covered; you will probably need to add a little more milk.

Serves 4 to 6

> **2-1/2 to 3 cups whole, 2% or 1% fat milk, or soymilk,
> just barely scalded with 3 bay leaves**
> **3 cups cooked rice**
> **Pinch salt**
> **1/2 cup cane sugar or demerara or turbinado sugar**
> **1/4 teaspoon freshly ground nutmeg or mace**
> **About 1 teaspoon freshly grated lemon zest**
> **1/2 teaspoon pure vanilla extract**

Add the rice, salt, and sugar to the 2-1/2 cups milk in a heavy-bottomed saucepan. Bring to a simmer over medium heat. Reduce heat, add the nutmeg and cook, just barely simmering, stirring occasionally, for 20 minutes. Depending upon how much it cooks down, you may or may not need to add the remaining 1/2 cup milk. Cool a spoonful, taste for sugar, and adjust if necessary. Add the lemon zest and cook for 5 minutes more, until thick and bubbling.

Remove from heat and stir in vanilla. Spoon into individual ramekins or custard cups and serve, or cool and serve at room temperature or refrigerate.

decadent vanilla crème brulee

One vanilla bean will give this *crème brulee* a delicious subtle flavor; however two beans will provide an intense vanilla taste which is quite decadent (especially considering the price of beans these days). Vanilla bean paste can be used rather than the whole beans— 1 tablespoon of paste is about equal to 1 whole bean.

Serves 6

    2 vanilla beans
    1-1/2 cups heavy cream
    1-1/2 cups whole milk
    6 extra-large egg yolks
    2 extra-large eggs
    2/3 cup sugar
    2 pinches sea salt
    Vanilla sugar

Preheat the oven to 350°F. Place 6 ramekins or custard cups in an ovenproof pan that can hold them without touching.

Cut the vanilla beans in half lengthwise. Using the tip of the knife, scrape most of the vanilla seeds from the pod, and put them into a heavy, non-reactive pan along with the pods. (If you are using the paste, add it now.) Add the cream and milk, stir, and bring to a simmer over low heat. Remove from heat, cover, and let stand to infuse for 1 hour.

Remove pods, scraping the excess from them into the cream. Gently reheat the infusion so that it is hot, but not simmering.

Meanwhile, beat the yolks and the eggs with the sugar in a bowl until light and fluffy. When the cream mixture is hot, add about 1/4 cup of it to the eggs and whisk well, then slowly add all of the remaining cream mixture to the eggs, whisking continuously.

Strain the mixture through a sieve and pour the mixture evenly into the prepared cups. Pour hot water into the pan to come halfway up the sides of the cups. Bake in a preheated oven for about 30 to 40 minutes. The custard should be set, with just barely a little shimmy in the center. Baking time will vary according to temperature, cups, etc.

Carefully remove the cups from the pan of hot water onto a baking rack and cool to room temperature. Refrigerate for at least 2 to 3 hours, or overnight. When ready to serve, sprinkle the tops of each crème brulee with about 2 teaspoons vanilla sugar and brown them under the broiler, paying close attention so they caramelize but don't burn. They should be about 3 to 4-inches from the heat and it will take about 5 minutes. There is a tool sold specifically for browning crème brulee—or a blowtorch also works—just be careful when using these tools. Remove from oven and let stand for 5 to 10 minutes before serving.

luscious lemon cream

This dessert is like a fluffy lemon mousse; however it is made without gelatin. It is easily prepared by making a lemon curd base, which can be made ahead and kept in the refrigerator. To prepare, just fold in freshly whipped lemon-scented cream. Serve simply in an elegant dessert dish, perhaps garnished with a lemon curl. If you ever have the opportunity to acquire Meyer lemons, this is heavenly when made with their exotic perfumey flavor. It would also be lovely served with fresh fruit or alongside angel food, genoise, or pound cake. Save the leftover curd for tarts, toast, scones or cake filling.

Makes about 2-1/2 cups

    1 cup whipping cream
    Handful of lemon verbena or lemon balm leaves
    3 medium lemons
    8 tablespoons unsalted butter, cut into 8 pieces
    1 cup plus 2 tablespoons sugar
    4 large eggs
    2 tablespoons sugar
    1 teaspoon pure vanilla extract

In a bowl combine the whipping cream with the lemon verbena or lemon balm leaves, bruising the leaves against the side of the bowl. Cover and refrigerate for at least 1 hour, or up to overnight.

Remove the zest from the lemons with a fine lemon zester or grater. Halve the lemons and squeeze the juice from them. Strain to remove the seeds; there should be a 1/2 cup juice.

Put hot water in the bottom of a double boiler. Combine the zest and juice in the top of a double boiler along with the sugar and butter. Place over medium heat and bring the water to a simmer. Stir the ingredients occasionally, until they are dissolved and blended, and hot to the touch.

In a separate bowl, beat the eggs well and pour them through a strainer into the top of the double boiler. Stir often while the mixture cooks, it will begin to thicken. It should get nice and thick in about 10 minutes—it should be like a thick white sauce or gravy—and sort of sheet off the spoon. Cook for a few minutes longer after it sheets. (if you want to use a candy thermometer, the temperature should be between 150-160°F, but this really isn't necessary).

Remove the top part of the double boiler from the bottom and stir the curd occasionally as it cools. Once you can put your hands on the outside of the pan, cover the top of the curd with wax paper and let cool to room temperature. Once cool, refrigerate until ready to use.

When ready to assemble, remove the herb leaves from the cream, squeezing the leaves to remove all of the essence. Using a hand or electric beater, beat the whipping cream, when it starts to thicken, add the 2 tablespoons of sugar. Beat until there are soft peaks and add the vanilla, and blend well. Fold 1-1/2 cups of the curd into the whipped cream, and reserve the remaining curd for another use. The lemon cream can be refrigerated until ready to use, or served in individual dishes. If kept refrigerated, you may need to whisk it a bit just before serving.

chocolate pudding with bay

This chocolate-rich pudding is redolent with the aroma of bay that lingers on your palate. Fresh bay leaves give the pudding a wonderful fragrance that you don't get when you use dried bay leaves. I generally harvest bay leaves and keep them in a plastic bag that is not sealed, on the door of the fridge for up to three months. I believe they have a better flavor if they are harvested a day or two ahead of when they are to be used; this way I always have them on hand. Most pudding is served cold—I prefer mine at cool room temperature so you really taste the flavors—this one is delicious even before it is chilled. This is also delectable when prepared with a handful of any of the mints—orange mint, spearmint, or peppermint.

Serves 6

> **2 cups half-and-half cream**
> **3 large fresh bay leaves or 2 dried bay leaves**
> **3 tablespoons cornstarch**
> **2/3 cup sugar**
> **2 pinches salt**
> **1/4 cup unsweetened cocoa**
> **1/2 cup milk**
> **3 ounces bittersweet or semisweet chocolate,**
>   **cut into small pieces**
> **1/2 teaspoon pure vanilla extract**

Heat the half-and-half cream with the bay leaves in a heavy-bottomed saucepan over medium heat. When the cream starts to bubble around the edges of the pan, remove from heat and cover. Let stand for 30 minutes.

After the bay has infused in the cream for nearly 30 minutes, combine the cornstarch, sugar, salt, and cocoa in a bowl and add the milk, whisk the contents together. Pour the mixture into the warm cream and place over moderate heat. Continue cooking and whisking as the pudding thickens.

When the pudding begins to bubble and come to a boil, stir and boil for 1 minute. Remove the pan from heat and whisk in the chocolate pieces until they are melted. Add the vanilla and stir well. Carefully remove the bay leaves and pour the pudding into six ramekins or custard cups.

Place the custard cups on a plate or pan and allow them to come to room temperature. Refrigerate until chilled; at least 30 to 45 minutes. Serve at cool room temperature and garnish with whipped cream if desired.

basil blueberry muffins

scones, muffins, & shortcakes

buttermilk cream scones with lemon herbs

pumpkin thyme scones

drop scones with rose petals & pistachios

basil blueberry muffins

lemon thyme muffin cakes

corn muffins with sage

strawberry shortcakes with herbs
& whipped cream

individual peach shortcakes
with bergamot flowers

buttermilk cream scones
with lemon herbs

The traditional way to eat a scone is first, split the scone in half. Next, spread each half with jam, and finally, place a generous spoonful of lightly whipped cream on top of each.

These delicious scones can be prepared for a special breakfast, brunch, tea party, or even served as dessert. Any of the lemon herbs work in this recipe—try lemon basil, lemon balm, lemon verbena, or lemon thyme. Sometimes I use pineapple or fruit-scented sage—kids particularly like their flavor. The candied ginger is a nice counterpoint, however if you don't have it on hand, try using minced dried apricots or currants.

Makes 8 large or 12 regular scones

    2-1/2 cups plus 2 tablespoons unbleached white flour
    3 tablespoons sugar
    3/4 teaspoon salt
    3 teaspoons baking powder
    1/2 teaspoon baking soda
    4 tablespoons unsalted butter
    1/4 cup finely chopped candied ginger
    1/2 cup buttermilk
    1/2 cup cream or milk
    1/4 cup freshly chopped lemon herb leaves
    1 heaping tablespoon lemon zest
    2 tablespoons fresh squeezed lemon juice
    About 1 tablespoon melted butter, optional
    About 2 teaspoons sugar, optional
    Marmalade or preserves
    Lightly whipped cream sweetened with a little sugar

Preheat the oven to 400°F. Combine the flour, sugar, salt, baking powder, and baking soda in a large bowl and blend thoroughly. With a pastry cutter or 2 kitchen knives, cut the butter into the dry ingredients until the butter is about the size of small peas. Add the candied ginger and stir well.

Stir the buttermilk and cream together with the lemon basil, zest, and lemon juice. Add the liquid to the dry ingredients and stir to form a soft dough.

Turn the dough onto a floured pastry marble or board, knead gently until it just comes together and shape into a ball. Press the dough with your hands to flatten the ball. Using a rolling pin, roll the dough into a round about 1-inch thick. Cut the dough with a sharp knife or pizza cutter into 8 or 12 pie-shaped wedges.

Place the scones about 1 inch apart on an ungreased baking sheet. Brush the tops of the scones with melted butter and sprinkle with sugar, if desired.

Bake the scones for about 18 minutes or until golden brown. Transfer the scones to a baking rack to cool slightly before serving. The scones are best served warm and right after baking.

I like to serve these with lightly sweetened whipped cream and lemon marmalade or a peach or ginger preserve.

pumpkin thyme scones

These scones are both sweet and savory, and need no adornment. They are best served warm with a pot of your favorite tea or a good, strong cup of joe. Dried cranberries can be used in place of fresh, however it is not necessary to toss them in the flour first. The scones may be cut into smaller square or diamond shapes if desired.

Makes 8 to 12 scones

> 2 cups unbleached flour
> 1 tablespoon baking powder
> 1/2 teaspoon salt
> 1/2 teaspoon ginger
> 1/2 teaspoon cinnamon
> 1/4 teaspoon freshly grated nutmeg
> 3 tablespoons plus 1 teaspoon sugar
> 4 tablespoons unsalted butter, cut into pieces
> 1/2 cup 2% milk or whole milk
> 1/2 cup unsweetened pumpkin puree
> 1 tablespoon plus 1 teaspoon fresh minced thyme
>   leaves, or 1 teaspoon dried thyme leaves, crumbled
> 3/4 cup fresh cranberries tossed with 1 tablespoon flour

Preheat oven to 400°F. In a mixing bowl, combine the flour, baking powder, salt, ginger, cinnamon, nutmeg, and 3 tablespoons of the sugar and stir to blend. Using a pastry blender or two knives, cut the butter into the dry ingredients until it is in pea-sized pieces.

Combine the milk with the pumpkin puree and thyme and blend well. Stir the milk and pumpkin mixture into the dry ingredients, along with the cranberries, until the dough starts to come together. Turn the dough out onto a lightly floured surface, gather it together, and knead lightly. Do not overwork the dough.

Flatten or roll the dough into a round about 1-inch thick. Cut the dough into 8 to 12 pie-shaped wedges. Sprinkle them lightly with the remaining teaspoon of sugar.

Place the scones on an ungreased baking sheet and place in the center of a preheated oven. Bake until the scones are golden on top, about 18 minutes. Cool on a baking rack for a few minutes and serve warm.

The scones can be wrapped in foil and gently reheated at 300°F for about 10 minutes.

drop scones
with rose petals & pistachios

These scones are a bit more exotic than your everyday scone and they are drizzled with a rose icing. If you prefer to serve them in a more traditional manner, pass a very lightly whipped cream and rose petal jelly as accompaniments.

Makes about 2 dozen scones

2-1/4 cups unbleached white flour
2 teaspoons sugar
3/4 teaspoon salt
2 teaspoons baking powder
1/2 teaspoon baking soda
2 to 3 pinches cinnamon
4 tablespoons unsalted butter
1/3 cup shelled pistachios, lightly toasted, and
    coarsely ground
1 cup heavy cream, or half-and-half cream
1 teaspoon rose water
A good handful of rose petals
1 cup confectioner's sugar
1 tablespoon rose jelly or 1 tablespoon red currant
    jelly mixed with about 1/2 teaspoon rose water
2 to 3 teaspoons water

Preheat oven to 425°F. Combine the dry ingredients in a large bowl and blend thoroughly. Using a pastry cutter or two knives, cut in the butter until the mixture resembles a coarse meal. Stir in the pistachios.

Stir the cream together with the rose water. Rinse the rose petals and pat them dry. Cut them into a chiffonade (thin ribbon-like shreds); there should be about 2 tablespoons. Stir them into the cream and add the liquid to the dry ingredients and stir to form a soft dough.

Drop the dough by the heaping tablespoonful onto an ungreased baking sheet. Bake the scones for 10 to 12 minutes or until golden brown. Prepare the icing while the scones are baking. Combine the confectioner's sugar, jelly, and 2 teaspoons water in a small bowl and whisk until smooth. Add another teaspoon water if icing seems too thick—it will melt a little if the scones are warm.

Remove the scones to a baking rack to cool slightly before drizzling them with icing. They are best served warm, right after baking.

If you want to prepare them in advance, cool them completely without icing and store them in an airtight container. Wrap them in foil and gently reheat in a 325°F oven for about 10 to 15 minutes. Drizzle the icing over them while they are warm.

basil blueberry muffins

This is a wonderfully delicious and fragrant muffin; it is sweet like cake. The addition of blue corn is fun and tasty—gives a bit of added texture and the corn is sweet—and I like the double blue emphasis. If you aren't familiar with blue cornmeal, try it and you will find its earthy taste is good in cornbread, muffins, and blue corn pancakes. You can use yellow or white cornmeal if you don't have the blue. I like a combination of lemon and cinnamon basil for the fragrance and flavor; the citrus and the spice go well with the blueberries. However, if you don't have both basils, either one can be used on its own and still make a tasty muffin.

Makes 1 dozen

    1/2 cup unsalted butter, melted
    1 2/3 cup unbleached flour
    1/3 cup blue cornmeal
    2 teaspoons baking powder
    1/2 teaspoon salt
    1/3 cup packed light brown sugar
    1/3 cup granulated sugar
    1/8 teaspoon freshly ground nutmeg
    1 generous cup blueberries
    1 cup milk
    2 extra large eggs
    Generous 1/4 cup minced lemon and cinnamon
        basil leaves

Preheat oven to 400°F. Use a little of the butter melted for the recipe to lightly brush the muffin tin. Set aside the remaining butter to cool.

In a mixing bowl, combine the flour, cornmeal, baking powder, salt, sugars, and nutmeg and toss well. Rinse the blueberries, pick them over, and drain well. Put them in a small bowl and toss them with 1 tablespoon of the flour mixture to coat them.

In a small bowl, lightly beat the eggs with a fork or a whisk, add the milk, and blend well. Stir in the melted butter and minced basil. Pour the liquid ingredients into the dry ingredients and stir to barely combine. Add the blueberries, folding them in gently, until they are just incorporated into the batter. Do not over mix.

Spoon the batter evenly into the muffin tins filling them about two-thirds full. Place in the middle of a hot oven and bake for about 20 minutes, until just golden brown, or a tester comes out clean. Cool in the tin for 5 minutes or so, loosen with a metal spatula and cool on baking racks or eat them warm.

lemon thyme muffin cakes

These are such rich, buttery, lemony moist muffins that they are really are more like cakes with a tender crumb and a pleasing herby aroma. They are good warm or at room temperature. Let them cool completely before storing in a cake tray.

Makes 12 muffin cakes

    1-1/2 cups unbleached flour
    1/2 teaspoon baking powder
    1/4 teaspoon salt
    3/4 cup milk
    2 tablespoons finely minced lemon thyme
    1 teaspoon finely grated lemon zest
    1/2 cup unsalted butter, softened
    1 cup and 3 tablespoons sugar
    2 large eggs
    1/2 teaspoon pure vanilla extract
    3 tablespoons lemon juice

Place cupcake papers or lightly butter and flour a muffin tin. Preheat oven to 350°F.

In a small bowl, combine the flour, baking powder, and salt, tossing lightly. In a measuring cup, add 1 tablespoon and 2 teaspoons of the thyme to the milk along with the zest and stir well.

Cream the butter in the bowl of an electric mixer on medium speed for about 3 minutes. Scrape down the sides and add 1 cup of the sugar and beat for 2 minutes, stopping to scrape down the sides. Add the eggs, one at a time, blending well after each one, scraping down the sides, if necessary. Beat for a few minutes until light and fluffy. Add the vanilla and beat for a minute.

On low speed, blend in half of the dry ingredients, add the milk mixture and mix well, and blend in the rest of the dry ingredients. Scrape down the sides and be sure the batter is well-blended. Spoon the batter evenly into the muffin tin.

Place in a preheated oven and bake for 25 minutes until the tops are just starting to turn golden brown and a tester comes out clean. While the muffin cakes are baking, combine the remaining 3 tablespoons sugar with the lemon juice and the remaining 1 teaspoon thyme and stir well to dissolve the sugar.

When the muffin cakes are done, remove the pan to a baking rack. Brush them with the lemon glaze; repeat another time if there is any leftover. Let them cool in the pan for 5 minutes and then remove them to cool on a baking rack.

corn muffins with sage

These are made with yellow cornmeal; however they can be made with blue or white cornmeal. The earthiness of the sage is a nice complement to the sweetness of the corn. The nutty crunch of sesame is tasty as well as nutritious.

Makes 1 dozen muffins

>   **Sesame seeds, optional**
>   **1-1/4 cups yellow cornmeal, preferably stone-ground**
>   **1 cup unbleached white flour**
>   **2 teaspoons baking powder**
>   **3/4 teaspoon salt**
>   **2 extra-large eggs, beaten**
>   **1-1/4 cups milk**
>   **1/4 cup vegetable or corn oil**
>   **3 tablespoons sorghum, molasses, or honey**
>   **2 tablespoons sage leaves, minced**

Preheat oven to 400°F and butter a muffin tin. Sprinkle about 1/2 teaspoon sesame seeds in the bottom of each tin, if desired.

Combine the cornmeal, flour, baking powder, and salt in a bowl and stir them with a wooden spoon to blend. In a small bowl mix the eggs, milk, oil, liquid sweetener, and sage. Pour the wet ingredients into the dry and stir until just blended.

Pour the batter into the buttered muffin tin. Bake for about 20 minutes, or until the tops are just golden brown. Remove from pan and serve immediately with butter, and molasses if desired.

strawberry shortcakes with herbs & whipped cream

Makes about eight, 3-inch shortcakes

topping

About 5 sprigs of lemon balm or orange mint
1 pint whipping cream
1 quart strawberries, rinsed, hulled and sliced
2 to 3 tablespoons grenadine syrup
Handful sweet woodruff sprigs, optional
Edible flowers for garnish

Bruise the herb sprigs, and put them in a bowl with the whipping cream, cover and refrigerate. Toss the berries in a bowl with the grenadine and handful of woodruff and stir to mix. Let stand for at least 30 minutes, or up to a few hours.

shortcakes

2 cups unbleached white flour
3 teaspoons baking powder
Scant 1/2 teaspoon salt
3 tablespoons sugar
6 tablespoons unsalted butter
1 cup half-and-half or whole milk
2 tablespoons orange mint or lemon balm, chopped fine
1 tablespoon unsalted butter, melted
1 tablespoon of sugar

Preheat oven to 425°F and lightly butter a baking sheet.

Combine the flour, baking powder, salt, and 2 tablespoons of the sugar in a bowl or processor. Using a pastry cutter or two knives, cut the butter into the mixture until it is a coarse meal. Add the half-and-half to the dry ingredients and mix until just blended. Add the chopped herbs—just mix them in—do not over mix.

Turn the dough onto a floured surface and knead 8 or 10 times. Roll or pat the dough to about 3/4 inch thick. Using a 3-inch cutter, cut out rounds, using all of the dough. Place the rounds of dough on the baking sheet, brush the tops with the melted butter, and sprinkle them with the sugar.

Bake the cakes in the center of the oven for about 12 to 14 minutes or until golden brown. Cool the shortcakes for at least 5 minutes before splitting them open; they are best served warm, but room temperature is fine.

While the cakes are baking, remove the herb sprigs from the whipping cream, add a heaping tablespoon of sugar and whisk until softly whipped.

To assemble the shortcakes, split them in half. Place a spoonful of berries on the bottom half with a bit of the juice. Add a dollop of whipped cream and place the top half on top. Repeat with the fruit and the cream and garnish the top with a berry slice and an edible flower. Serve immediately.

shortcake dough ready to be baked

57

individual peach shortcakes with bergamot flowers

If you don't have bergamot, try using orange mint, lemon balm, lemon verbena, fruit-scented sage, cinnamon basil, or anise hyssop. Leaves can be used, but the flowers are really prettiest for garnish.

Makes about eight, 3-inch shortcakes

topping

6 to 8 very ripe peaches, peeled and sliced
1 tablespoon lemon juice
1 to 2 tablespoons sugar
2 to 3 tablespoons bergamot flowers &/or leaves
1 recipe shortcakes (from strawberry shortcake recipe)
Whipping cream or vanilla ice cream

Toss the peaches in a bowl with the lemon juice, sugar, and half of the bergamot flowers &/or leaves. If the fruit is tart use the larger amount of sugar; if it is sweet, use less. Reserve the remaining flowers for garnishing the dessert.

Preheat oven to 425°F and lightly butter a baking sheet. Prepare the recipe for shortcakes as instructed in the strawberry shortcake recipe, except use bergamot flowers &/or leaves in place of the orange mint or lemon balm. Bake according to recipe.

Cool the shortcakes for at least 5 minutes before splitting them open; they are best served warm, but room temperature is fine.

To assemble the shortcakes, split them in half. Place a spoonful of fruit on the bottom half with a bit of the juice. Add a dollop of whipped cream or a spoonful of ice cream and place the top half on top. Repeat with the fruit and the cream and garnish the top with a few peach slices. Scatter the reserved blossoms over the desserts and serve immediately.

tropical fruit salad with vanilla mint syrup

fruit

herbs that partner with fruit

tropical fruit salad with vanilla mint syrup

berries with sweet woodruff

peach crisp with lavender

strawberry rhubarb cobbler

pears poached with rosemary
& chestnut whipped cream

fresh fruit tarts with bergamot

summer fruit trifle with lemon herb syrup

rustic apple tart with bay leaves

simple yet exotic oranges & dried fruit

herbs that partner with fruit:

angelica—These stems have a slightly woody, bitter, resinous flavor with a hint of fruit, and are usually candied for a garnish to decorate desserts; the aromatic leaves are good chopped for fruit salads, with citrus and rhubarb.

basil—Lemon and cinnamon basil add citrus and cinnamon flavor to summer fruit salads, sorbets, and pear conserves. Genoa green and spice basil work well with citrus and tomato in preserves.

bay—A fresh leaf lends citrus and balsam-like flavor with a hint of vanilla and nutmeg, to custards baked with fruit, and also left to rise in sweet bread dough with dried fruits.

bergamot—A favorite herb for the stone fruits of summer like apricots, peaches, plums, apples, and berries; this herb has a perfumey, tea-like flavor. Use in fruit salads, stewed or poached fruit, and in making jellies or preserves. The red flower blossoms are a tasty garnish with the same perfume.

borage—The delicate star-shaped flowers, with their clean cucumber taste are used fresh and candied for garnishing desserts, punches, and wine cups.

chervil—This mild, anise-flavored herb with a hint of citrus is best used fresh with mild-flavored fruits such as melons, apricots, plums, peaches, papaya, kiwi, and fruit salads.

coriander—The nutty and highly citrus-flavored seed is used in baked goods, with apples, bananas, pears, cherries, apricots, and peaches. The cilantro leaf, which has grassy and resinous taste with a hint of citrus, goes best with citrus fruits; oranges, tangerines, grapefruits, pineapples, and complements coconut and pomegranate.

fennel—The anise-flavored seed can be baked in fruit desserts made with apples, pears, and rhubarb and the sweet feathery leaves can be used with fresh fruit.

geraniums—The distinct and unique leaves range in fragrance and flavor from rose and nutmeg to lemon and peppermint. They are used to flavor cakes, tarts, and jellies made with apricots, every type of berry, currants, and apples, and in citrus sorbets. The leaves and flowers make fragrant garnishes.

lavender—Use only the blossoms in the kitchen, do not use the foliage of this highly perfumed, flowery herb. It goes well with raspberries, blueberries, blackberries, currants, and peaches. Its flavor is more delicate when used with dairy products as in cream sauces, custards, and ice creams.

lemon balm & lemon verbena—Both of these highly aromatic, lemon-flavored herbs add sweet and citrus tastes to desserts. Verbena is stronger in citrus oil and therefore has more concentrated flavor than balm, so adjust accordingly in a recipe. Use in custards, pies, cakes, and jellies. Chopped fresh it is good in fruit salads, sorbets, and berry fools.

mint—There are many mints—apple, orange, pineapple, spearmint, and peppermint—all culinary favorites. Choose peppermint if you want more menthol, spearmint if you prefer it sweeter, and orange mint if you want that flavor of Earl Grey tea. Mint is good with any fruit, and is a good companion to all of the berries, grapes, melons, peaches, and plums. It adds a refreshing tingle to fruit salads, sorbets, pies, fools, and jellies. It also works well when baked with apples and pears.

rose—The unmistakable perfume of roses can lend an exotic quality to desserts, however no two roses taste alike and some are downright bitter or sour, so be sure to taste before using. Rose petals, rosehips, and rosewater are used in making candy, cookies, syrups, jellies, and frostings; they should be used with mild-flavored or citrus fruits in order to savor their delicate scent.

rosemary—Since this herb has such a strong resinous and piney flavor it should not be used with mild-tasting fruits. It is an herb that is great with red wine—use it for poaching or macerating apples, pears, oranges, cranberries, and dried fruits. It adds good flavor to mulled wine, tea, and cider.

thyme—This well-rounded herb has a flavor that is sweet and savory and is tasty with apples and pears, baked, stewed, or macerated in compote, also tasty in grape and cranberry jelly. Lemon thyme and orange thyme have   citrus flavors and are less savory, and can be added to fruit salad; but they tend to lose some of their citrus dimension when cooked.

sage—Use cold-weather fruits like apples and pears with this earthy, musky, slightly camphorus-tasting herb, stewed, in a sauce or fritters, or baked in bread or cake.

sweet cicely—The leaves and flowers of this anise-flavored herb are best used fresh, in fruit salads, although it is good stewed with pears or apples.

sweet woodruff—This traditional herb of spring goes best with seasonal fruits—strawberries and rhubarb. Its delicate scent of hay-and-vanilla goes well with most berries and is delicious used in infusions and macerations with white and sparkling wines. The tiny white blossoms are a lovely garnish on desserts and in the punch bowl.

tropical fruit salad
with vanilla mint syrup

This syrup works with practically any combination of fruit; however, I especially like it with the tropicals. Under ripe and tasteless fruit can be rescued by macerating it in this syrup. The fruit salad is a light and refreshing dessert; the use of the vanilla bean makes these fruits seem exotic. Sometimes, I add a garnish of lime zest or mint leaves, cut into chiffonade to this salad.

Serves 8 to 10

> 1 cup water
> 1/4 cup sugar
> 1/2 vanilla bean
> 1 handful of fresh mint leaves, bruised
> Few strips of lime zest
> 1 to 1-1/2 tablespoons freshly squeezed lime juice
> 1 firm ripe mango or papaya, peeled, seeded,
>   and cut into dice
> 1 small, ripe cantaloupe or honeydew, seeded,
>   and cut into dice
> 1 ripe pineapple, peeled, cored, and cut into
>   bite-sized pieces

Make the flavored fruit syrup by combining the water, sugar, and vanilla. Bring the contents of the pan to a boil, reduce heat, and simmer for 10 minutes. Remove from heat, add the mint and zest, and let cool. When cooled to room temperature, strain the syrup and stir in the lime juice. At this point the syrup can be stored in the refrigerator for up to 5 days.

Toss the fruit together in a large bowl. Pour about 1/2 the syrup over the fruit. Toss the mixture well, add more syrup to taste. Cover the fruit and chill it for at least 1/2 hour before serving. Serve at cool room temperature.

berries with sweet woodruff

This recipe can be made with any one of the following berries or a combination of them—strawberries, raspberries, and blueberries. Use a good quality, not-too-sweet Prosecco or Asti Spumante sparkling wine. The sweet vanilla perfume of the woodruff infused in the tart/sweet bubbly with the sweet and tart berries makes an elegant and lovely light dessert.

Serves 6

> **2 cups ripe strawberries**
> **1 cup raspberries**
> **1 cup blueberries**
> **1 handful sweet woodruff leaves**
> **1 bottle Prosecco or Asti Spumante**
> **1 large handful sweet woodruff blossoms**

Rinse the berries and drain well. Halve the strawberries if they are large. Put the berries and woodruff leaves in a shallow bowl and pour 2 to 3 cups of Prosecco or Asti Spumante over them, so they are just covered.

Cover the dish with plastic wrap and refrigerate for 1 to 2 hours, stirring once or twice. Remove from refrigerator about 15 to 20 minutes before serving. Remove sweet woodruff sprigs and discard. Transfer the berries and liquid into a serving dish and toss lightly with the woodruff blossoms or serve in individual serving dishes. Pour a splash of Prosecco or Asti into each dish as it is served to give it a bit of fizz.

peach crisp with lavender

There is nothing to compare with fresh, ripe peaches at the height of the summer. Their luscious fragrance, flavor and sweetness are enhanced by the perfume of lavender flowers. Serve with lightly whipped cream and a lavender bloom.

Serves 8

6 cups sliced ripe peaches, about 2-1/2 pounds
1 tablespoon lemon juice
About 1/3 cup sugar
1 tablespoon and 2 teaspoons cornstarch
1 scant tablespoon fresh lavender flowers or 1 teaspoon dried lavender flowers
1 cup unbleached flour
1 cup packed light brown sugar
12 tablespoons unsalted butter, cut into pieces
1/8 teaspoon salt
Few grindings of nutmeg

Preheat oven to 400°F and butter a 2-1/2-quart baking dish. Combine the peaches, lemon juice, sugar, cornstarch, and lavender flowers in a bowl and toss well. If the peaches are tart add a little more sugar. Transfer the peach mixture to the baking dish and spread evenly.

Combine the flour, brown sugar, salt, and nutmeg in a bowl and stir to blend. Cut the butter into the crisp ingredients with a pastry blender until just blended. Spread the mixture over the fruit and bake in preheated oven for about 30 minutes, until the crisp is golden brown and the peaches are bubbling. Serve warm or at room temperature.

strawberry rhubarb cobbler

Sweet woodruff doesn't have much of an aroma when picked fresh, but when it is dried, infused, or cooked it imparts a homey flavor, rather like adding a taste of vanilla and a scent of fresh mown hay. Serve this dessert with vanilla ice cream or fresh whipped cream, garnished with a sprig of sweet woodruff.

Serves 6

fruit

4 cups rhubarb, scrubbed and cut into 1/2-inch dice
4 cups fresh strawberries, halved
About 1 cup sugar
10 or 12 sprigs sweet woodruff about 3 inches long
2-1/2 tablespoons unbleached flour

Place rhubarb, berries, sugar, and sweet woodruff in a saucepan and bring to a simmer. Reduce heat, stir, and cook for 3 to 5 minutes. Remove from heat and set aside. Let the mixture cool a bit and remove the woodruff sprigs, then stir the 2-1/2 tablespoons of flour into the fruit.

dough

1 2/3 cups unbleached flour
2-1/2 tablespoons sugar
1/2 teaspoon salt
2 teaspoons baking powder
6 tablespoons cold unsalted butter, cut into pieces
1 cup milk

Preheat oven to 425°F and butter a 2-1/2-quart baking dish.

Combine the flour, sugar, salt, and baking powder in a bowl. Using a pastry cutter or two knives, cut the butter into the flour mixture until it is in pea-sized lumps. Add the milk to the flour mixture and mix with a fork until just blended.

Transfer the fruit to the buttered dish. Drop the dough from large spoonfuls over the fruit. Bake the cobbler for 15 minutes, then reduce oven to 350°F. Bake for 15 to 20 minutes more, or until the fruit is bubbling and the dough is turning golden brown. Serve warm or at room temperature.

pears poached with rosemary & chestnut whipped cream

My friend Carolyn Dille and I developed this elegant autumn or winter dessert when we owned and operated a catering business. It is one of my favorites and is definitely a grown-up dessert.

Serves 6 to 8

fruit

6 to 8 firm, ripe pears, Bosc or D'anjou are good varieties
About 3/4 to 1 bottle full-bodied red wine
1 cup port wine
2 or 3 pieces lemon peel
2 3-inch sprigs fresh rosemary
1/3 cup sugar

Peel the pears leaving the stems on. Combine the rest of the ingredients in a stainless or enamel pan large enough to hold the pears comfortably. The pan should be deep enough so that the wine covers at least two-thirds of the pears when they are standing.

Bring the wine to a boil and reduce to a simmer. Add the pears and poach them for about 25 minutes, turning them occasionally so that they color evenly, until they are tender but firm. Remove them from the liquid and cool on a platter. Remove rosemary sprigs and reduce the poaching liquid by half and cool to room temperature.

chestnut cream

**10 to 12 ounces fresh chestnuts, or canned chestnuts
packed in water
Milk to barely cover, about 1 cup
3-inch sprig fresh rosemary
3 tablespoons mild honey
1/2 pint whipping cream
Sugar**

Slit the fresh chestnuts and put them in a nonreactive saucepan. Cover the chestnuts with about 2 inches of water and bring to a boil. Reduce heat and simmer for about 30 minutes. Drain and rinse the chestnuts. When cool enough to handle remove the skins from the chestnuts. If using canned chestnuts, just rinse and drain them.

Place the chestnuts in a small nonreactive saucepan with enough milk to barely cover them. Add the honey and rosemary and simmer for 10 to 15 minutes. Cool the chestnuts for abou 15 minutes and remove the rosemary sprig. Put the chestnuts through the fine blade of a food mill or puree them with the milk in a food processor.

Whip the cream, adding a little sugar to taste; fold the chestnut puree into the whipped cream. Refrigerate the cream until ready to assemble the dessert; remove about 10 minutes before serving time.

To serve, stand the pears on individual dessert plates and drizzle them with the reduced poaching liquid. Spoon a generous dollop of chestnut cream alongside each pear. Serve immediately.

fresh fruit tarts with bergamot

These little tarts can be made with whatever fruit is in season; as long as it is perfectly ripe. My personal favorites for making these tarts are apricots, peaches, and plums, peeled and thinly sliced, or strawberries, raspberries, and blueberries. If you like, a few of these can be combined to make a colorful array, or all one type of fruit can be used. Orange mint or bay leaves can be used in place of the bergamot.

Makes 18 2-1/2-inch tart shells.

pastry dough

1-3/4 cups unbleached white flour
2 pinches salt
1-1/2 tablespoons sugar
12 tablespoons unsalted butter (1-1/2 sticks)
3 tablespoons cold water
1 egg white, lightly beaten, for glazing

Combine flour, salt, and sugar in a food processor and pulse to blend. Cut the butter into 12 pieces and add it to the processor; process until the mixture resembles a coarse meal. Add water all at once while processing, and process until the mixture just starts to come together. Do not over process.

Turn the dough onto a pastry marble or board and gather the dough together. Flatten the dough into a disk, wrap in plastic, and refrigerate for at least 30 minutes. (At this point the dough can be wrapped well and frozen for up to 4 weeks, if desired.)

Use regular size muffin tins (2-1/2-inch) to form these tarts or use small tart pans, if you have them. Using your hands, pinch off small pieces of dough and press them into the tins to form the bottoms of the tart shells. Then pull off pieces and press the dough evenly to form the sides. The dough should be pressed just a bit above the rim of the pans since it will slump a little during baking.

Cover the tart shells with plastic or foil and place in the freezer for at least 30 minutes. The tart shells can be tightly wrapped and frozen until ready to use or baked after 30 minutes.

Preheat oven to 400°F. Bake the shells for about 8 to 10 minutes or until pale golden brown. About halfway through baking, prick the bottoms of the shells with a fork, if they are puffing up. Remove the tart shells from the oven and brush the insides very lightly with egg white and bake for another 2 minutes until just golden.

Cool the shells in the tins on baking racks until lukewarm. Gently remove them from the tins and finish cooling on baking racks. When completely cool, store in an airtight container until ready to fill.

custard with bergamot

1-1/2 cups milk
4 or 5 3-inch sprigs bergamot or orange mint
1/3 cup sugar
1 tablespoon and 1 teaspoon cornstarch
Pinch salt
3 extra-large egg yolks
1/4 teaspoon pure vanilla extract

Scald the milk with the bergamot, bruising the sprigs against the side of the pan with the back of a wooden spoon. Let steep for 30 to 60 minutes, until the milk has cooled. Remove the herb sprigs, squeezing them to extract their flavor.

Combine the sugar, cornstarch, and salt in a small bowl and add it to the milk. Place the pan over medium heat and whisk the ingredients well. Beat the egg yolks lightly. When the milk mixture starts to get hot, add about 1/3 cup to the egg yolks and whisk well. Pour the egg mixture into the pan and whisk well. Continue cooking and whisking as the mixture thickens. When the first bubble appears in the custard, time 30 seconds, stirring constantly, and then remove the pan from the heat.

Pour the custard into a bowl to cool, stirring every 5 minutes or so with a whisk, to release the steam. When the custard is lukewarm, stir in the vanilla, cover the top with wax paper and refrigerate until well chilled. (The custard can be made a day ahead.)

assembling the tarts

About 1/2 cup red currant jelly or 1 cup apricot preserves,
4 or 5 small apricots or plums or 3 small peaches, or 1 pint
raspberries, strawberries, or blueberries
Small bergamot or orange mint leaves for garnish

Melt the red currant jelly or apricot preserves in a small saucepan over low heat. The apricot preserves will have to be strained to remove large pieces of pulp.

Peel the apricots, plums, or peaches and slice them thinly. Rinse the berries and pick them over. If the strawberries are large, they will need to be sliced.

Spoon a heaping tablespoon of custard into each tart shell. Arrange the fruit slices or berries on top of the custard. Brush the melted jelly or preserves over the fruit. Garnish with a leaf, if desired. Keep the prepared tarts in a cool place or refrigerate them. These are best assembled at the last minute, but they can be prepared up to 2 hours in advance.

summer fruit trifle
with lemon herb syrup

Traditionally most trifles are made with sponge cake or lady fingers, custard and jam—this trifle has been brought up to date—it is lighter and fresher, and quite delicious. I've used an angel food cake, fresh fruit of the season, and captured the flavor of the herbs of summer in a simple syrup. Substitute the freshest fruit available—apricots, nectarines, strawberries, blackberries, raspberries, or currants. If you don't have time to bake the cake, buy one. Any of the lemon herbs—lemon balm, lemon verbena, lemongrass, or lemon basil are wonderful—or use a combination of them.

Makes 1 large trifle; about 24 servings (recipe can be easily halved)

10-inch angel food cake (see cakes)
1 recipe lemon herb syrup (see miscellaneous)
About 8 ripe peaches
2 pints blueberries
2 pints raspberries or strawberries
2 tablespoons grenadine syrup
1 quart whipping cream
1/2 cup sugar
1-1/2 teaspoons pure vanilla extract
Lemon herbs for garnish

You will need a large, preferably clear glass, serving bowl. Slice the angel food cake into 3/4-inch slices; cut the slices into about 3/4-inch squares. Once the syrup has cooled, squeeze the essence from the herbs and remove them.

Peel and pit the peaches and slice them thinly. Put them in a bowl and pour a little of the syrup over them so that they do not turn dark. Rinse and pick over the blueberries and add them to the bowl. Toss with a little more syrup.

Rinse the raspberries and transfer them to a separate bowl. If you are using strawberries, rinse, hull, and slice them. Toss the berries with the grenadine; if you don't have it, use the herb syrup.

Whip the cream, adding the sugar a few tablespoons at a time. Add the vanilla towards the end. The cream should have soft peaks.

Place a layer of peaches and blueberries (using half of them) in the bottom of the bowl with some of the syrup. Cover them with about a quarter of the cake squares. Spoon about one-fourth of the whipping cream over the cake. Place half of the berries over the cream, add another quarter of the cake, and then another fourth of the cream. Use the rest of the peaches and blueberries, another quarter of the cake, and fourth of the cream. The final layer is berries, the remaining cake, drizzle about 1/4 to 1/2 cup syrup over all, and spoon on the remaining cream.

Refrigerate until about 30 minutes before serving. Allow to stand at room temperature to bring out the flavor. Garnish with lemon herb leaves, or a few berries, or some edible flowers.

rustic apple tart with bay leaves

This rustic-looking tart is homey as it is tasty. The bay adds a hint of citrus and spice to the apples. It needs no adornments, however it is yummy when served with vanilla or butter pecan ice cream, or whipping cream. Sometimes I serve it with very thin slices of sharp white cheddar cheese. I like it the next day for breakfast with the tang of plain yogurt. The crust is easy to handle. Do not eat the bay leaves.

Makes 8 servings

pastry

1-3/4 cup unbleached white flour
1/2 cup whole-wheat flour
1 tablespoon sugar
2 pinches salt
10 tablespoons unsalted butter
1/4 to 1/3 cup ice water

Mix the dry ingredients together in a bowl. In the same bowl with two knives or a pastry cutter, or in a food processor with the steel blade, cut the butter into the flour. Add the smaller amount of ice water and stir with a fork, or pulse to mix. If a ball forms, don't add the rest of the water, otherwise add it so that the dough comes together.

Turn the dough onto a floured surface and gather it into a ball. Work quickly and gently, kneading just a few times until the dough comes together. Place the dough on a piece of wax paper or plastic wrap, flatten it, and wrap it. Refrigerate the dough while preparing the apples.

filling

3 or 4 fresh bay leaves
6 apples, peeled
1 lemon, zest removed, and halved
1 cup packed light brown sugar
1 teaspoon cinnamon
1/2 teaspoon mace
1/4 teaspoon each: allspice & cloves
1-1/2 tablespoons flour
2 tablespoons unsalted butter, cut into small pieces

Place the bay leaves in a large bowl. As you peel and slice the apples into the bowl, squeeze just a little lemon juice over each one. When the apples are sliced, sprinkle the brown sugar, spices, and flour over them and add the remaining lemon juice and zest. Toss well to coat. Set aside, while rolling out the crust. Preheat the oven to 425°F.

Roll the dough out on a lightly floured surface into an oval about 15 x 18-inches. It doesn't have to be exact or perfect—this is freeform. Gently fold the dough in half to lift it onto a baking sheet and open it to lay flat. Spread the apple mixture in the center of the dough, leaving about 2-inches of dough showing all around. Dot the apples with the butter. Fold the edges in all around so that they overlap the apples, and the apples in the center are showing.

Bake in a hot oven for 10 minutes, and reduce heat to 375°F. Bake for 35 to 40 minutes more. The crust should be golden brown and the apples should be tender, but not mushy, when pierced with a knife tip. Remove baking sheet to cool on a baking rack. If you cut the tart when it is hot it will be runny. Serve warm or at room temperature.

simple yet exotic oranges & dried fruit

This mouthwatering dessert is light, yet sweet and satisfying. The oranges are refreshing to the palate, the dried fruits add sweetness, the flower waters are subtly exotic, and the fennel seed aids in digestion besides giving an interesting flavor nuance, and the pistachios add a surprise crunch, nuttiness, and salt. Use all oranges in this recipe, or for a little more texture and a different flavor, try replacing two of the oranges with apples. I use navels because they are seedless, however, temples, tangelos, tangerines, and clementines are also tasty. Crisp apples that are both tart and sweet—Nittany, Gala, Jonagold, or Winesap—work well here. The seeds of a pomegranate sprinkled over the top of this salad make a jewel-like garnish.

Serves 6

1 cup fresh-squeezed or not-from-concentrate orange juice
1/2 cup pitted dates, sliced crosswise
1/3 cup chopped prunes
1 teaspoon orange flower water
1/2 teaspoon rosewater, optional
20 fennel or anise seeds, bruised
6 oranges or 4 oranges and 2 apples
1/4 cup shelled pistachios
pomegranate seeds, optional

Pour the orange juice into a large measuring cup, or a jar with a lid. Add the chopped dates and prunes, orange flower and rosewater, and the bruised fennel or anise seed. Stir the ingredients with a fork or put the lid on the jar and shake well to combine ingredients. Let the sauce stand at cool room temperature while you prepare the fruit. The sauce can be made a day or two in advance and refrigerated.

Peel the oranges and halve them lengthwise. Cut them crosswise into slices. If using apples, cut them in half, remove the core, and slice into half moon shapes. Arrange the orange and apple slices in a shallow bowl or deep platter. Pour the sauce over the arranged fruit and let stand for at least 20 to 30 minutes before serving. Sprinkle the pistachios over the fruit just before serving.

spice cake with lemon thyme cream cheese frosting

cakes

lemon poppy seed cake

nectarine & plum cake with bergamot

sage & apple upside-down cake

herbal tea loaf

lemon verbena angel food cake
with lemon syrup

spice cake
with lemon thyme cream cheese frosting

orange cake with dried cherries & pecans
& orange mint buttercream

buttermilk chocolate cake with peppermint
& minted chocolate buttercream

ricotta cheesecake with sweet marjoram

lemon poppy seed cake

This rich, buttery, lemony moist cake has a pleasing herby aroma with a tender crumb. A friend of mine, Lisa Yockelson is a wonderful baker and this recipe is an adaptation of her Lemon-Poppy Seed Pound Cake from *A Country Baking Treasury*. The lemon herbs make a fragrant addition; however, if you don't have them, it is still quite delicious.

Makes a 10-inch bundt cake

3 cups unbleached flour
1 teaspoon baking powder
1/2 teaspoon baking soda
1/2 teaspoon salt
1-1/2 cups milk plus 1 tablespoon lemon juice
About 2 tablespoons finely minced lemon balm,
     lemon thyme, or lemon verbena, optional
Generous tablespoon finely grated lemon zest
1 cup unsalted butter, softened
2 cups sugar
4 extra-large eggs
1 teaspoon pure vanilla extract
1/2 teaspoon pure lemon oil or 1 teaspoon lemon extract
1/3 cup poppy seeds
About 1/4 cup lemon juice
About 1/4 cup sugar

Generously butter and flour a bundt pan. Preheat oven to 350°F.

In a small bowl, combine the flour, baking powder, baking soda, and salt, sift ingredients together once, and set aside. In a measuring cup, combine the lemon herbs, with the milk and lemon juice and add the zest, stir well.

Cream the butter in the bowl of an electric mixer on medium speed for about 3 minutes. Scrape down the sides and add the sugar and beat for 2 minutes, stopping to scrape down the sides. Add the eggs, one at a time, blending well after each one, scraping down the sides, if necessary. Beat for a few minutes until light and fluffy. Add the vanilla and lemon oil or extract, beat for a minute.

On low speed, blend in the dry ingredients in three parts and the milk mixture in two parts, starting with the dry ingredients, and alternating with the wet, mix well. Scrape down the sides and fold in the poppy seeds, blending well. Pour and spoon the batter evenly into the pan.

Place in a preheated oven and bake for about 1 hour until the top is golden brown and a tester comes out clean. While the cake is baking, combine the remaining 1/4 cup lemon juice with the 1/4 cup sugar and stir well to dissolve the sugar.

When the cake is done, remove the pan to a baking rack and let cool for 5 minutes. Turn the cake out onto a baking rack and brush with the lemon glaze; repeat another time if there is any leftover. Let the cake cool on a baking rack. It will keep for 5 days, tightly covered, or freeze for up to a month.

nectarine & plum cake
with bergamot

This is not your typical peach cake with fruit slices arranged on the top. Although the fruit is placed on top of the batter, the batter is so light the fruit has a tendency to fall. Some of the fruit stays on top and some sinks to the bottom—this results in a very moist cake with fruit and herbs throughout.

All nectarines or all plums can be used to make the cake but I like the combination of the two fruits together. If you don't have bergamot leaves, use the same amount of orange mint, or any of the lemon herb leaves for an equally delicious flavor.

Makes a 9 x 13-inch cake

fruit

> **3 medium-sized ripe nectarines**
> **3 large, ripe but firm, plums**
> **1/4 cup sugar**
> **2 to 3 tablespoons lemon juice**
> **3 3-inch sprigs bergamot or orange mint**

Peel the nectarines and plums. Slice the nectarines into twelfths and the plums into eighths and put them in a shallow bowl. Sprinkle the fruit slices with the sugar and lemon juice and toss with the herb leaves, bruising the leaves against the side of the bowl to release their essence. Let the fruit and herbs macerate, stirring occasionally, while preparing the cake batter.

cake

14 tablespoons unsalted butter
5 extra-large eggs
2 extra-large egg yolks
1 1/3 cups sugar
2 cups unbleached white flour
1/2 teaspoon salt
Finely grated zest of 1 lemon
20 bergamot leaves (1/4 cup cut into chiffonade)

Butter and flour a 9 x 13-inch pan and preheat the oven to 375°F. Melt the butter over low heat and set aside to cool.

With an electric mixer, beat the eggs, yolks, and sugar in a bowl, until the mixture becomes pale yellow and fluffy. This should take about 5 minutes.

Sift the flour with the salt. Gently fold the flour, one-third at a time, into the egg mixture. Carefully fold the melted butter, one-third at a time, into the batter. When the batter is thoroughly blended, fold in the lemon zest.

Pour the batter into the prepared pan, spread evenly, and strew the herbs over the batter. Arrange the fruit slices on top (the leftover nectar is for the cook to sip).

Bake for 40 minutes until pale golden brown, the cake pulls slightly away from the pan, or a tester comes out clean. Do not overcook. Cool the cake in the pan on a baking rack. The cake can be cut into squares and served from the pan, or the cake can be turned out onto a baking rack, inverted, and served from a platter. Serve alone, or accompanied by fresh whipped cream, garnished with bergamot flowers and leaves.

sage & apple upside-down cake

I've always had a fondness for upside-down cakes; my grandmother used to make a good one with cherries in the center of the pineapple rings. I suppose as a kid I liked that what was on the bottom of the pan turned out to be on the top. So I make upside-down cakes with all sorts of different toppings; I also like that they are baked in an iron skillet. Both apples and pears are a great combination with sage; this is a simple, moist, not-to-sweet, eat-any-time-of-day kind of cake. Rosemary or savory would also work in this recipe. I use a 10-inch skillet, if you use a 9-inch it will be a thicker cake and if you use an 11-inch it will be a thinner cake, the baking time will vary 5 to 10 minutes.

Serves 8 to 10

> **4 tablespoons unsalted butter**
> **1/2 cup packed dark brown sugar**
> **2 large tart apples, cored, peeled, sliced thin and tossed with 1 tablespoon lemon juice**
> **12 to 15 fresh sage leaves**
> **2-1/4 cups unbleached flour**
> **1/2 teaspoon salt**
> **2 teaspoons baking powder**
> **1-1/2 teaspoons baking soda**
> **1/2 teaspoon fresh ground nutmeg**
> **4 tablespoons unsalted butter, softened**
> **1 cup sugar**
> **3 extra-large eggs**
> **1-1/2 cups nonfat buttermilk**
> **About 8 sage leaves, stacked and cut crosswise into very thin chiffonade (about 1-1/2 tablespoons fresh)**

88

Melt 4 tablespoons butter in a 10-inch iron skillet over medium low heat. Add the brown sugar, stir until it is dissolved; it should look like thick chocolate syrup. Continue to cook until the mixture just starts to bubble, then remove promptly from heat.

Arrange the apple slices and whole sage leaves close together in the skillet on top of the butter and sugar. Arrange extra apples slice around the sides of the skillet. Preheat the oven to 375°F. Combine the flour, salt, baking powder, baking soda, and nutmeg together in a bowl.

In a mixing bowl, beat the softened butter, add the sugar and blend well. Add the eggs, one at a time, beating well after each addition. Add the buttermilk and mix until blended.

Add the dry ingredients to the bowl and the sage chiffonade; beat until the batter is just mixed. Stir to be sure the batter is smooth. Pour the batter over the apples in the skillet.

Bake in the center of the oven for 15 minutes. Lower the heat to 350°F and bake for about 25 minutes more. The cake is done when it is golden brown, the edges pull slightly from the sides, and a tester comes out clean.

Remove the cake from the oven and carefully run a metal spatula around the edges. Place a cake plate over the skillet and carefully turn the cake out onto the plate. It should come out easily; rearrange any apple slices or sage leaves if they get out of place. If there is any excess topping in the skillet, scrape it onto the cake. Let the cake cool for at least 20 minutes before serving. It is good served slightly warm or at room temperature.

herbal tea loaf

This cake has a tender crumb, is not as heavy as a pound cake, and it is good for slicing and serving alone for tea or with fruit and whipped cream, or for dipping in fondue. You can flavor this cake in many ways. If you are using herb leaves such as mint or lemon balm, use 2 tablespoons finely minced leaves for a mild flavor and 3 tablespoons for a stronger taste. If you are using flowers like lavender, scented geraniums or anise hyssop, you will need 1-1/2 to 2 teaspoons fresh flower blossoms or 1/2 teaspoon dried flowers.

Makes a 9 x 5 x 3-inch loaf

> **2 cups unbleached flour**
> **1 teaspoon baking powder**
> **1/4 teaspoon salt**
> **to 3 tablespoons minced herb leaves or 1-1/2 teaspoons edible flower blossoms**
> **1/2 cup milk**
> **8 tablespoons unsalted butter, softened**
> **1 cup sugar**
> **3 extra-large eggs**
> **1 teaspoon pure vanilla extract**

Preheat the oven to 350°F. Butter and flour a 9 x 5 x 3-inch loaf pan.

Sift the flour into a bowl with the baking powder and salt. Set aside. Mix the herbs into the milk and let stand.

In a large bowl, cream the butter. Beat the sugar with butter. Beat the eggs in one at a time until the mixture becomes light and fluffy, about 3 minutes. Add the vanilla and blend well.

Add the flour alternately in 3 parts with the milk. Pour the batter into the pan, spreading it evenly. Bake for 45 to 50 minutes. The loaf is done when the top is golden brown, the edges pull away slightly, and a cake tester comes out clean.

Cool in pan for 10 minutes before turning the cake out of the pan to finish cooling on a rack. When cool, cut into 1-inch squares for dipping into fondue.

lemon verbena angel food cake with lemon syrup

A homemade angel food cake should be light yet toothsome. This cake is that and more—the hint of lemon herb adds a nice taste—but is not overpowering. The syrup gives the outer crust of the cake a burst of tart and sweet lemon flavor.

Serves 10 to 12

- 1-1/4 cups cake flour
- 1-1/2 cups sugar
- 1-1/2 cups egg whites (whites from 12 to 14 extra-large eggs)
- 1-1/4 teaspoons cream of tartar
- 1/4 teaspoon salt
- 1/4 teaspoon pure vanilla extract
- 2 tablespoons fresh squeezed lemon juice
- Zest from 1 lemon
- 1/3 cup packed fresh lemon verbena or lemon balm leaves, minced fine

Preheat oven to 375°F. Sift the flour with 3/4 cup sugar two times and set aside.

Beat the egg whites in the bowl of an electric mixer until foamy. Sprinkle the cream of tartar and salt over the whites and beat until soft peaks form.

Add remaining 3/4 cup sugar to the egg whites 2 tablespoons at a time, beating after each addition just enough to blend. Fold in the vanilla, lemon juice, and zest.

Fold the flour and sugar mixture into the beaten egg whites about 1/4 cup at a time. Add the lemon verbena or balm and fold just enough to blend. Turn the batter gently into a 10-inch ungreased angel food cake pan with removable bottom. Bake on the bottom oven rack at 375°F For 10 minutes and reduce heat to 350°F and bake for 30 minutes more, or until the cake is very high and golden brown on top. If the top of the cake browns too fast towards the end of baking, cover it loosely with foil.

Remove cake from oven and invert pan over bottle to cool for 2 hours before removing cake from pan.

lemon syrup

3 tablespoons fresh squeezed lemon juice
Zest from 1 lemon
4 tablespoons sugar
2 tablespoons water
About 12 to15 lemon verbena or lemon balm leaves

In a small nonreactive saucepan combine the lemon juice, zest, and sugar, water, and herb leaves. Heat over medium heat, stirring occasionally, bruising the herb leaves against the side of the pan, with the back of a spoon. Bring to a simmer and cook for about 3 minutes. Remove from heat and let cool to room temperature.

Place the cake on a serving plate. Remove the herb leaves from the syrup, squeezing to remove excess liquid. With a spoon, drizzle the syrup over the top of the cake and down the sides. Garnish with lemon verbena or balm leaves, if desired.

spice cake with lemon thyme & cream cheese frosting

This tasty spice cake has a pleasant hint of thyme combined with the spices; the addition of nuts gives the cake more depth of flavor; they are optional. The frosting is soft rather than butter-cream consistency. You can leave the cake in the pan to cool and spread the frosting over the top, or turn the cake out of the pan onto a platter when it cools, and frost it. Garnish with sprigs of thyme or toasted nuts sprinkled. I like to use the lemon-scented thymes, orange balsam, or Provencal for this recipe. They are sweeter and have less thymol and carvacrol than other thymes which will impart a more savory flavor. The same amount of sweet marjoram or three fresh bay leaves can be used in place of the thyme.

Serves about 15 three-inch squares or 24 two-inch squares

- 1/2 cup milk scalded with 15 to 20 sprigs of lemon thyme
- 2-1/4 cups unbleached flour
- 1-1/4 teaspoon baking powder
- 1 teaspoon baking soda
- 1 teaspoon freshly grated nutmeg
- 1 teaspoon cinnamon
- 1/4 teaspoon cloves
- 1/4 teaspoon ginger
- 3/4 teaspoon salt
- 12 tablespoons unsalted butter, softened
- 1-1/2 cups sugar
- 3 extra-large eggs, separated
- 3/4 cup nonfat buttermilk
- 2 tablespoons fresh minced thyme leaves
- 1/3 cup chopped walnuts, pecans, or hazelnuts, toasted

Preheat the oven to 350°F. Lightly butter a 13 x 9 x 2-inch baking pan and dust lightly with flour. Set the scalded milk and thyme aside to cool.

In a bowl, sift the flour with the baking powder, baking soda, nutmeg, cinnamon, cloves, ginger, and salt and set aside.

In a large bowl, whip the butter with an electric mixer for a minute or so. Add the sugar and beat until fluffy. Add the egg yolks, one at a time, beating well after each addition, stopping to scrape down the sides of the bowl.

Remove the thyme from the scalded and cooled milk and add 1/4 cup of the milk to the buttermilk, reserving the other 1/4 cup for the icing. Alternately add the flour mixture in three parts with the milk mixture in two parts to the butter mixture, beginning and ending with the flour, the batter will be stiff. In a separate bowl, beat the egg whites until they are stiff. Fold them into the batter in three parts, adding the chopped thyme and walnuts with the last addition and blend well.

Pour and scrape the batter into the prepared pan. Bake for about 40 minutes until a tester comes out clean and the cake starts to pull away slightly from the sides of the pan. Cool the cake in the pan on a baking rack.

cream cheese frosting

4 ounces cream cheese, softened
2 tablespoons unsalted butter, softened
About 2 tablespoons reserved thyme-flavored milk
2-1/2 cups confectioners' sugar
1 tablespoon pure maple syrup
Few dashes nutmeg

In a large bowl, cream the cream cheese with the butter with an electric mixer for 2 or 3 minutes. Add the confectioners' sugar, about 1/2 cup at a time and blend well after each addition. Add the milk 1 tablespoon at a time, alternating with the sugar. Scrape down the sides of the bowl occasionally so the frosting will mix evenly. You will probably need about 2 to 2-1/2 table-spoons of the milk, you will not use all of it. Add the maple syrup and nutmeg and beat on high speed to whip and thicken the frosting. The icing will be soft.

When the cake is cool, you can frost it in the pan or gently loosen the cake with a spatula and turn it out onto a serving platter. Spread the frosting over the top of the cake, it will be too soft to adhere to the sides. Garnish the cake with thyme sprigs or toasted walnuts.

spice cake with lemon thyme cream cheese frosting

97

orange cake
with dried cherries & pecans
& orange mint buttercream

The idea for this cake came to me because I always look forward to the fresh crop of citrus and dried fruits and nuts in the autumn months. Any kind of fresh orange or tangerine can be used in making this cake and dried cranberries work just as well as the dried cherries. The orange mint imparts a wonderful flavor to this rich cake and buttercream, *Monarda didyma* could also be used here, but be sure that it is the red-flowered one which has a more tea-like flavor. Many of the other monardas are savory and taste like oregano and that is not the flavor you want in this cake!

Serves 10 to 12

> **1-1/2 cups milk scalded with 1 cup chopped**
>   **orange mint leaves**
> **Zest from 2 large oranges**
> **About 1/2 cup fresh squeezed orange juice**
> **1/2 cup dried cherries or cranberries (3 ounces)**
> **2/3 cup toasted pecans, chopped coarse , tossed with**
>   **2 teaspoons flour**
> **2-1/2 cups unbleached flour**
> **1/2 cup cake flour**
> **1-1/2 teaspoons baking powder**
> **1/2 teaspoon salt**
> **1 cup unsalted butter, softened (2 sticks)**
> **2-1/4 cups sugar**
> **4 extra-large eggs**

Preheat the oven to 350°F. Lightly grease two 9-inch layer cake pans, line the bottoms with a circle of wax paper, and dust lightly with flour. Set the scalded milk and orange mint aside to cool. Soak the dried berries in the orange juice.

In a bowl, sift the flour with the cake flour, baking powder, and salt and set aside.

In a large bowl, whip the butter with an electric mixer for a minute or so. Add the sugar and beat until fluffy. Add the eggs, one at a time, beating well after each addition. Strain the orange juice from the berries and add the juice, reserve the berries.

Remove the orange mint from the scalded and cooled milk and measure 1 cup of the milk for the cake batter, reserving the other 1/2 cup for the buttercream. Alternately add the flour mixture in three parts with the milk in two parts to the butter and egg mixture, beginning and ending with the flour, stopping to scrape down the sides of the bowl when necessary. Fold 2 tablespoons of the zest, berries, and nuts into the batter.

Divide the batter evenly into the prepared pans. Bake for 30 to 35 minutes until a tester comes out clean and the cake starts to pull away slightly from the sides of the pan. Cool the pans on a baking rack for 5 to 10 minutes, remove the cakes from the pans and remove wax paper. Turn the cakes right-side-up to cool.

orange buttercream

8 tablespoons unsalted butter, softened
1 pound box confectioners' sugar
About 1/3 cup reserved milk flavored with orange mint
About 2 tablespoons orange zest, finely chopped

In a large bowl, whip the butter with an electric mixer for a minute or so. Add the confectioners' sugar, about a cup at a time and blend well after each addition. Add the milk 1 or 2 tablespoons at a time, alternating with the sugar. Add the orange zest. Scrape down the sides of the bowl occasionally so the buttercream will mix evenly. You will probably need about 5 to 6 tablespoons of the milk, you will not use all of it. The buttercream should be a nice spreading consistency.

Assemble the cake with the buttercream, spreading it between each layer, over the sides and top of the cake. Garnish the cake with orange mint leaves if desired.

buttermilk chocolate cake with peppermint & minted chocolate buttercream

This layer cake is fudgey and moist with a nice hint of peppermint. The buttercream is a light chocolate with refreshing mint flavor. I like peppermint here because it is stronger in flavor, however, spearmint can be used. My family likes this cake on the day after it has been made when the mint has permeated the entire cake. I usually refrigerate it and take it out of the refrigerator 15 to 20 minutes before serving so that it is at cool room temperature. It can be garnished with a circle of fresh or candied mint leaves arranged on the top.

Serves 10 to 12

1 cup milk scalded with 1 cup packed peppermint leaves
2-1/2 cups unbleached flour
1/2 cup unsweetened cocoa powder
1 teaspoon baking soda
1/2 teaspoon baking powder
1/2 teaspoon salt
10 tablespoons unsalted butter, softened
1-3/4 cup sugar
4 extra-large eggs
1 teaspoon pure vanilla extract
**2 squares (2 ounces) unsweetened chocolate, melted
   and cooled**
1 cup nonfat buttermilk
1/2 cup fresh chopped peppermint leaves

Preheat the oven to 350°F. Lightly grease two 9-inch layer cake pans, line the bottoms with a circle of wax paper, and dust lightly with flour. Set the scalded milk and mint aside to cool.

In a bowl, sift the flour with the cocoa, baking soda, baking powder, and salt and set aside.

In a large bowl, whip the butter with an electric mixer for a minute or so. Add the sugar and beat until fluffy. Add the eggs, one at a time, beating well after each addition. Add the vanilla and the chocolate and blend well, stopping to scrape down the sides of the bowl.

Remove the mint from the scalded and cooled milk and add 1/2 cup of the milk to the buttermilk, reserving the other 1/2 cup for the buttercream. Alternately add the flour mixture in three parts with the milk mixture in two parts to the chocolate mixture, beginning and ending with the flour. Add the chopped mint and blend well.

Divide the batter evenly into the prepared pans. Bake for 25 minutes until a tester comes out clean and the cake starts to pull away slightly from the sides of the pan. Cool the pans on a baking rack for 5 to 10 minutes, remove the cakes from the pans and remove wax paper. Turn the cakes right-side-up to cool.

chocolate mint buttercream

8 tablespoons unsalted butter, softened
2 squares (2 ounces) unsweetened chocolate,
**   melted and cooled**
1 pound box confectioners' sugar
Reserved 1/2 cup mint-flavored milk

In a large bowl, whip the butter with an electric mixer for a minute or so. Add the chocolate and blend well. Add the confectioners' sugar, about a cup at a time and blend well after each addition. Add the milk 1 or 2 tablespoons at a time, alternating with the sugar. Scrape down the sides of the bowl occasionally so the buttercream will mix evenly. You will probably need about 4 to 6 tablespoons of the milk, you will not use all of it. The buttercream should be a nice spreading consistency.

Assemble the cake with the buttercream, spreading it between each layer, over the sides and top of the cake.

ricotta cheesecake
with sweet marjoram

In southern Europe, especially in Italy, they make cheesecake with ricotta cheese. It has a different texture and is less dense than New York-style cheesecake. I decided to try and capture the essence of sweet marjoram in this recipe—be sure that you use *Origanum majorana* for it's sweet aroma and flavor—which suggest citrus, flowers, thyme and a hint of resin. The torte is tasty on its own, however, it is also delicious served with seasonal fruit such as berries, sliced peaches, or a compote of honey and dried figs with a few sprigs of marjoram.

Makes a 9-to-9 1/2-inch cheesecake

crust
   1 cup whole almonds
   1 cup unbleached flour
   Large pinch salt
   1/4 cup confectioners' sugar
   10 tablespoons cold unsalted butter, cut into pieces

filling
   3/4 cup sugar
   1/3 cup sweet fresh marjoram leaves
   Zest of 1 lemon
   4 extra-large eggs
   3 cups ricotta cheese
   1 teaspoon pure vanilla extract
   1/2 teaspoon lemon extract or pure lemon oil

Generously butter a 9 to 9-1/2-inch spring form pan. Preheat the oven to 400°F.

To make the crust, grind the almonds in a food processor until they are nearly fine. Add the flour, salt, and confectioner's sugar and pulse until blended. Add the butter and pulse until it is blended—it will not become a cohesive dough—more like moist sand. Do not over process. Transfer the mixture to the spring-form pan and press the dough about 2-inches up the sides of the pan and evenly over the bottom. Bake in the preheated oven for 10 minutes. Remove to a baking rack to cool. Reduce oven to 350°F.

To prepare the filling, combine the sugar and the marjoram leaves in the processor and pulse until the marjoram is finely minced. Add the lemon zest and pulse a few more times.

Beat the eggs in a bowl with a fork. Stir in the sugar mixture, add the ricotta and extracts and blend well. Pour the filling into the baked crust. Bake for exactly 1 hour. The cake will be set, but the center will just be a little soft. Remove to cool on a baking rack. Once cool, refrigerate until ready to serve. Remove from refrigerator about 15 to 20 minutes before serving so that it isn't really cold.

bitter & semisweet chocolate with salted pistachios & chipotle

chocolate

herbs & flowers that partner with chocolate

chocolat

european-style hot chocolate with mint

bittersweet chocolate fondue with peppermint

two chocolate fondue with lavender flowers

chocolate rose-scented soufflé

bitter & semisweet chocolate
with salted pistachios & chipotle

favorite chocolate sauce

bittersweet chocolate truffles with orange mint

mendiants

herbs & flowers
that partner with chocolate:

angelica
anise hyssop
basil—anise, cinnamon, and genoa green
bay
chiles
coffee
damiana
garlic
ginger
lavender flowers
mints—orange mint, peppermint, and spearmint
oats
rose
rosemary
scented geraniums—rose, coconut, mint, nutmeg, and orange
tarragon
tea
vanilla
seeds: anise and coriander

candied edible flowers
that partner with chocolate:

clove pinks
lilacs
pansies
rose petals
scented geraniums
violets

chocolat

This seductive beverage was inspired by the one prepared in the movie *Chocolat*. Rich, dark, and smooth this hot chocolate is subtly uplifted with a hint of vanilla and the spice of ground chile. (Do not use chili powder—the mix of spices with cumin and oregano. Use pure ground red chile pepper like the rich pasilla, chile negro, or ancho, or combine them.) The word chocolate comes from the Aztec and Mayan *"xocoatl"* which translates as bitter drink. These Indians who believed it gave them power and sexual energy mixed it with chiles, vanilla and spices.

European hot chocolate is prepared with cream and melted chocolate rather than milk and cocoa, and served with whipped cream. Experience the best of both worlds—this recipe is very rich—or you can make it with all milk. If you use bittersweet chocolate, you will need the larger amount of sugar, with semi-sweet use the lesser amount. Try just a few pinches of chile or about 1/4 teaspoon and then taste—and add more if desired—I like this recipe with about 1/2 teaspoon so it warms the tongue. For those who don't prefer the heat of chiles, cinnamon can be substituted in its place.

Serves 2, or 4 small demitasse

- 2 cups half-and-half cream or 1 cup half-and-half cream and 1 cup milk
- 2 to 3 tablespoons sugar
- 2 ounces semisweet or bittersweet chocolate, cut into pieces
- 2 tablespoons unsweetened cocoa powder
- 1 teaspoon pure vanilla extract
- 1/4 to 1/2 teaspoon pasilla or ancho chile powder
- 1 pinch mace

In a heavy-bottomed nonreactive saucepan, combine the cream, sugar, chocolate pieces, and cocoa powder. Place over medium heat and stir with a whisk. Keep stirring with a whisk until the sugar is dissolved and the chocolate is melted; do not allow the hot chocolate to boil.

Turn the heat to low and whisk so there is some froth on top. Remove from heat and stir in the vanilla and 1/4 teaspoon ground chile powder & a pinch of mace, let sit a minute or two, whisk, and taste for seasoning. Adjust with a little more chile if necessary and serve. Serve hot with whipped cream if desired.

The chocolate can be cooled and refrigerated and reheated the next day. I keep it in the fridge and reheat it—I like to drink it in small amounts in little demitasse cups.

european-style hot chocolate with mint

Rich, dark, and smooth, this hot chocolate is subtly uplifted with the flavor of mint. I like peppermint; however, spearmint or orange mint would also be good. In the cafés in Europe, hot chocolate is usually prepared with melted chocolate rather than cocoa, and served with a dollop of whipped cream on top. If you want to gild the lily here, you can add about a tablespoon of the mint syrup to the whipping cream after you have whipped it.

Serves 3 or 4
- **1 cup water**
- **1/2 cup sugar**
- **6 sprigs peppermint about 4 to 5-inches long**
- **2 cups half-and-half cream**
- **2 ounces semisweet or bittersweet chocolate, cut into pieces**
- **1/4 cup unsweetened cocoa powder**
- **Lightly sweetened and whipped cream, optional**

Combine the water, sugar and mint in a small saucepan, bruising the mint against the side of the pan with a spoon. Place over moderate heat and bring to a boil. Cover, remove from heat and let stand for at least 30 minutes. Remove the mint leaves and squeeze them into the syrup to extract their flavor. This syrup can be made ahead and refrigerated.

In a heavy-bottomed saucepan, combine the cream, chocolate, cocoa powder, and 1 cup mint syrup. Place over medium heat and stir with a whisk. Keep whisking until the chocolate is melted; do not allow it to boil. Turn the heat to low and whisk so there is some froth on top. Serve hot with whipped cream. It can be refrigerated and reheated.

bittersweet chocolate fondue with peppermint

This recipe is for those who like dark chocolate; it is not overly sweet and is especially good with the peppermint. A delicious variation is to use orange mint in place of the peppermint and Grand Marnier or another orange-flavored liquor instead of the cognac. My particular favorite item for dipping in dark chocolate fondue is cubes of sourdough walnut bread.

Serves 6 to 8

> **12 ounces good quality bittersweet chocolate**
> **1 cup heavy cream**
> **1/4 cup packed peppermint leaves, rough chopped**
> **1 to 2 tablespoons cognac, dark rum, or water**
> **Cubes of angel food or pound cake, banana slices, whole strawberries or Bing cherries, chunks of kiwi fruit or pineapple, slice of apple, marshmallows, graham crackers, or thin salted pretzels**

In a small heavy saucepan, combine the mint with the cream and just barely bring it to a simmer. Remove from the heat and steep for 30 to 60 minutes. Pour the cream through a strainer to remove the herbs and set aside.

Break or chop the chocolate into about 1-inch pieces. In a heavy-bottomed saucepan, combine the chocolate with 3/4 cup of the cream and melt over medium-low heat. Stir or whisk occasionally and do not allow the mixture to simmer. As the mixture melts check the thickness and add more cream for the proper consistency. It shouldn't be too thick or runny; it should coat a piece of fruit when dipped in it.

Stir in the cognac or rum and cook over medium-low heat for a minute or two before serving. Transfer the fondue into a fondue pot with a small burner under it. The heat should be low, just enough to keep the fondue warm; do not let it bubble. If you need to remove the pot from the heat for awhile and it thickens or becomes grainy, just add another tablespoon of cream and use a whisk to blend it in.

two chocolate fondue
with lavender flowers

The flavor of this fondue is a bit exotic, geared more toward the herbally aware or adventurous fondue crowd. Anise hyssop flowers can be substituted, or 2 teaspoons Earl Grey tea leaves—infuse them in the cream as you would the lavender flowers. Strawberries were voted the most popular dipping item for this flowery fondue.

Serves 6 to 8

> **6 ounces milk chocolate**
> **4 ounces good-quality bittersweet chocolate**
> **3/4 cup heavy cream**
> **6 lavender flower spikes or 3/4 teaspoon dried lavender flowers**
> **1 tablespoon Kirshwasser (cherry brandy), brandy, or water**
> **Cubes of angel food or pound cake, banana slices, whole strawberries or Bing cherries, chunks of kiwi fruit or pineapple, slice of apple, marshmallows, graham crackers, or thin salted pretzels**

In a small heavy saucepan, combine the lavender with the cream and just barely bring it to a simmer. Remove from the heat and steep for 30 to 60 minutes. Pour the cream through a strainer to remove the herbs and set aside.

Break or chop the chocolate into about 1-inch pieces. In a heavy-bottomed saucepan, combine the chocolate with 1/2 cup + 1 tablespoon of the cream and melt over medium-lowheat.

114

Stir or whisk occasionally and do not allow the mixture to simmer. As the mixture melts check the thickness and add more cream for the proper consistency. It shouldn't be too thick or runny; it should coat a piece of fruit when dipped in it.

Stir the kirsch or brandy in and cook over medium-low heat for a minute or two before serving. Transfer the fondue into a fondue pot with a small burner under it. The heat should be low, just enough to keep the fondue warm; do not let it bubble. If you need to remove the pot from the heat for awhile and it thickens or separates, just add another tablespoon of cream and use a whisk to blend it in.

chocolate rose-scented soufflé

Originally, I tried preparing this recipe with rose water, but the flavor was not strong enough. Rose syrup is good in this recipe, however, cooking down fresh organic rose petals takes longer than the following simple syrup. By all means, try rose syrup if you have some on hand.

To make rose geranium syrup, combine 1 cup water with 1 cup sugar and about 10 or 12 rose geranium leaves in a small saucepan, bruising the leaves against the side of the pan with a spoon. Place over moderate heat and bring to a boil. Cover, remove from heat and let stand for at least 30 minutes. Remove the leaves and squeeze them into the syrup to extract their flavor. This syrup can be made ahead and kept in the refrigerator for up to 3 months. You can make other herb-flavored syrups in the same manner. Orange mint, peppermint, spearmint, or anise hyssop would be good in this recipe; use about five 4 or 5-inch sprigs in place of the geranium leaves.

Serves 6 to 8

- 1/2 cup half-and-half cream
- 4 ounces semisweet chocolate, broken into pieces
- 1 ounce unsweetened chocolate, broken into pieces
- 1/4 cup sugar
- 2 pinches salt
- 5 extra-large eggs, separated
- 1/4 cup rose or rose geranium syrup
- Whipping cream
- Organic rose geranium flowers, rose petals or
  candied rose petals (see crystallized edible flowers)

Preheat the oven to 375°F. Generously butter six 1-cup ramekins or custard cups and sprinkle lightly with sugar.

Combine the cream, chocolate, sugar, and salt in a heavy-bottomed saucepan. Place over medium low heat. Whisk the chocolate as it melts to make a smooth mixture. Remove from heat when the chocolate is completely melted. Cool slightly.

Beat the 5 yolks, one at a time, into the chocolate mixture. Whisk the rose geranium syrup into the chocolate, 1 tablespoon at a time. In a separate bowl, beat the egg whites until stiff but not dry.

Whisk about a cup of the egg whites into the chocolate mixture. Then pour the chocolate mixture into the whites and fold until just blended. Pour the mixture into the prepared dishes and bake in the lower half of the oven for 12 minutes, until they are set.

While the soufflés are cooking, whip about 1/2 cup whipping cream with 1 tablespoon of sugar until almost stiff. Whisk in about 1 tablespoon rose syrup, taste; add a bit more if desired.

Remove the soufflés from the oven. Scatter a few fresh rose petals or rose geranium flowers over the soufflés if you have them, or garnish each soufflé with a candied rose petal. Serve the soufflés immediately and pass the whipping cream. (You have about 5 to 7 minutes to serve the soufflés before they start to deflate.)

If you have leftover soufflés, you can refrigerate them and eat them the next day. Their texture will be denser, but they are still tasty served at cool room temperature.

bitter & semisweet chocolate with salted pistachios & chipotle

This is my idea of the perfect candy confection, I find it titillating. The combination of good quality bitter chocolate combined with the salted pistachio with a hint of ground smoky chile that lingers in the back of my palate is my idea of a perfect bite. I am a chile head, so this might not appeal to everyone. When prepared with unsalted pistachios—this tastes flat to me—salt with the bitter and sweet is part of the formula. I have converted a number of pure chocolate lovers to adulterating their chocolate with this recipe. In fact, I have a few devotees who call me for a fix every now and then. I like this with a chocolate that is somewhere between 60 to 75% cocoa.

Tempering chocolate is not hard—it is just precise (a bit fussy)— and really only requires a little patience. The reason for tempering chocolate is that it brings down, or stabilizes the crystalline structure in chocolate and it also gives it a shiny luster and a snap when it breaks. Chocolate only needs to be tempered when it is going to be used on its own, say to make candy, molded, or used as a coating. There are many methods for doing this — you can even do it in the microwave. I'm just going to give you the simple basics.

Makes a generous pound block of nut bark

> **1 pound bitter or semisweet chocolate or a combination, broken into pieces or chopped coarse**
> **About 1 1/2 cups salted, shelled pistachios**
> **1/2 teaspoon ground chipotle powder**

Place a piece of parchment paper on a baking sheet and spread the pistachios out in one layer fairly close together.

Put 3/4 pound of the chocolate in the top of a double boiler and reserve the rest. Place the double boiler over medium heat and bring the water in the bottom to a simmer, then reduce heat so that it is hot, but not simmering. Stir the chocolate as it melts. Do not allow any steam or water to get in the chocolate or it will freeze up.

Using a candy thermometer, the temperature should reach over 100°F, but not more than 120°F, in order to melt all of the chocolate. When the chocolate is melted, remove from the bottom of the double boiler (sit the pot on a towel—careful not to get any water in the chocolate!) and stir.

Stir the chocolate and let it begin to cool. Drop a handful of the reserved chocolate into the melted chocolate and stir until it melts. The idea is to cool the melted chocolate and reintroduce the beta crystals as you stir in the reserved tempered chocolate. Repeat with the rest of the chocolate, a handful at a time, the temperature should reduce to 90°F or below.

Add the ground chipotle powder after the last bit of reserved chocolate is added to the tempered chocolate. Taste for pungency before you pour the chocolate over the nuts and add more if desired. It should give a nice warm hot zing on the back of the palate once savored. The amount of nuts will tame the pungency just a little; however, the salt brings out both the bitterness and heat.

If you touch the chocolate it should not feel warm. If you dip the tip of a clean knife in it, it should start to set up in 1-1/2 to 3 minutes. Once any of these occur, the chocolate begins to set and the crystals set faster, so prepare to pour the chocolate.

Pour the chocolate evenly back and forth across the pistachios, just covering them. If there is any chocolate left, fill in the holes or thin spots. There should be enough to just cover the 1-1/2 cups of pistachios. Gently tap the pan on a hard surface to spread the chocolate evenly. Put in a cool place and allow to harden.

Once hardened, turn the pistachio bark over on the parchment paper (hands and fingers will leave dull prints so handle as little as possible) and whack with the heavy handle of a kitchen knife to break into pieces. It is best to wrap chocolate in foil for storage (or pack into tins) and store at cool room temperature.

favorite chocolate sauce

This sauce is so quick and easy and really tasty—and it is actually good for you too! Dutch-process cocoa is less bitter, but you can use whatever you have on hand. Use wherever chocolate sauce is needed—it is good on ice cream of any flavor, in a black-and-white ice cream soda, on a brownie sundae, or as a base to make hot chocolate. Add it to a glass of milk, and stir well, to make a seriously delicious glass of chocolate milk.

Makes about 1 cup

1/2 cup good-quality cocoa
1/2 cup pure maple syrup
1/2 teaspoon pure vanilla extract

Combine the cocoa with the syrup in a jar and mix with a fork until the cocoa is dissolved. Add vanilla, stir, cover with lid and label. The sauce will keep in the fridge for months (if it lasts that long!); remove about 15 minutes or so before using so it won't be quite as cold and thick.

bittersweet chocolate truffles with orange mint

Truffles are not hard to prepare and they make a delicious, decadent dessert, end to a meal, or special gift. You could make these with peppermint, lavender, basil, or even tarragon. However, I find orange mint delightful here with a subtle, yet slightly exotic fragrance and taste. For these truffles, buy the best chocolate you can find for the best flavor.

Makes about 3 dozen large truffles or 5 dozen small truffles

1 1/3 cups heavy cream
About 8 4-to 5-inch sprigs orange mint
1 pound bittersweet chocolate (70% cocoa)
Unsweetened cocoa

Combine the whipping cream with the orange mint in a -quart, heavy-bottomed nonreactive saucepan. Bruise the leaves against the side of the pan with a wooden spoon. Bring the contents of the pan to a simmer remove from heat. Cover, and let the herbs steep in the liquid for 30 minutes.

Break the chocolate up into small pieces or chop it in a food processor.

Remove the herb sprigs from the cream, squeezing them to extract their essence. Gently reheat the cream until almost simmering. Remove from heat and stir the chocolate into the cream. Stir vigorously until the cream and chocolate are blended.

Transfer the mixture into a mixing bowl and cool. It will take from 1 to 2 hours for the ganache to cool and set. To speed this process you can place the mixture in the refrigerator or over a bowl of ice until it is cool, but do not allow it to become cold and hard. Whisk or beat for a few minutes until it has firmed to spreading consistency. If it isn't firm enough chill a little more. If it is too hard, sit it over a bowl of warm water for a minute.

Using a teaspoon, scoop out the ganache and drop it into a saucer with cocoa powder. Lightly coat the truffles in the cocoa and place in a storage container between layers of wax paper. If you prefer, you can quickly roll the ganache into rounds before dipping them in the cocoa. I like the rough, organic look of dropped truffles. Store the truffles in the refrigerator, tightly covered, for up to two weeks. Serve at cool room temperature.

mendiants

I actually saw these confections in the movie *Chocolat* and then came across them in an expensive food catalog, where I noted that they were called *mendiants*. I immediately rifled all of my chocolate and dessert cookbooks and finally found them in Alice Medrich's *Bittersweet* (which I might add is a great book of delectable bittersweet chocolate recipes).

I have made many mendiants in all sizes and with all sorts of garnishes. Personally, I like small, bite-sized ones. Although a big, 6-or 8-inch mendiant is an impressive presentation and can be broken into pieces for serving. Be inspired with your combination of toppings—here is your chance to be creative. Probably I like them best with just one or two of the following ingredients, occasionally a combination of three will work. If you use too many or too weird combinations you lose the essence and beauty of the alchemy of flavors. Most of the candied herb leaves or flowers I prefer alone with the chocolate. Use the ground spices in small amounts—just a light dusting.

Here are a few right-on combos: ground chile with pistachio, almond, or toasted, salted pumpkin seed; candied grapefruit peel and ground star anise or anise seed; candied orange peel and cinnamon or cardamom; dried cherries and hazelnuts with a dust of nutmeg—you get the idea. Think of flavors that you like and sense would work well together.

1/2 pound tempered chocolate makes about 40, 2-inch mendiants (see bitter & semisweet chocolate with salted pistachios and chipotle for tempering chocolate instructions)

Spread a couple of baking sheets with parchment. Have all of your topping ingredients prepared and ready. This is fun to do with a friend, because you have to work fairly quickly once your chocolate is tempered.

candied herb leaves and edible flowers

Small crystallized leaves of anise hyssop, basil, lemon balm, orange mint, peppermint, and spearmint, blossoms of lilacs, johnny-jump-ups, and violets, petals of pansies and roses.

ground spices or seeds

Whole anise or fennel seed, freshly ground cardamom, chiles, cinnamon, clove, coffee, coriander, ginger, mace, nutmeg, or star anise.

candied herbs, spices, and fruit

Slivers of candied angelica, ginger, grapefruit and orange peel.

dried fruits

Blueberries, currants, halved cherries, cranberries, or raisins, very thinly slivered apricots, dates, figs, pears, prunes, or strawberries.

nuts and seeds

Halved, slivered or chopped almonds, hazelnuts, pecans, pine nuts, pistachios, walnuts, pumpkin or sunflower seeds.

I make the mendiants in small batches, using a small ladle, I spoon about 5 or 6 small rounds of chocolate onto the parchment (sort of like spacing cookies). Then I quickly decorate them before they begin to harden (the toppings won't stick if the chocolate hardens). Then I pour another little batch and decorate, etc. Keep them in a cool place (not the refrigerator) until they harden and then pack them in tins, between wax or parchment paper. They will keep for a month or two.

chocolate ice cream with anise-flavored herbs

ice creams & sorbets

lemon basil ice cream

chocolate ice cream with anise-flavored herbs

peppermint ice cream with mini chocolate chips

cantaloupe sorbet with summer herbs

citrus sorbet with opal basil

pineapple sorbet with pineapple sage blossoms

lemon basil ice cream

This velvet-textured ice cream has a wonderful taste of lemon and basil and leaves a delightful perfume lingering on the palate. It can also be prepared with anise or cinnamon basil, but the lemon is ethereal.

Makes about 1 quart

> **2 cups whipping cream**
> **1 cup milk**
> **3/4 cup sugar**
> **12 three to four-inch sprigs lemon basil**
> **3 extra-large egg yolks**

Combine the whipping cream, milk, sugar, and basil in a heavy-bottomed nonreactive saucepan. Bring the contents of the pan to a simmer remove from heat. Let the herbs steep in the liquid for 30 minutes. Remove the herb leaves, pressing to extract their essence.

Return the pan to gently reheat over low heat. Lightly whisk the eggs in a small bowl and add about 1/4 cup of the warm cream to the eggs and whisk, add another 1/4 cup and whisk again. Pour the egg and cream mixture into the saucepan and cook, stirring constantly, until the custard lightly coats a metal spoon, about 5 minutes.

Strain the cream mixture into a bowl, and chill. Freeze according to manufacturer's instructions.

chocolate ice cream
with anise-flavored herbs

This creamy chocolate ice cream becomes nearly exotic when flavored with a hint of anise or licorice. Anise or Thai basil are delicious in this recipe or it can also be prepared with other licorice-flavored herbs like tarragon or anise hyssop. If you don't prefer an anise flavor, then try mint or cinnamon basil, which are always a good choice with chocolate.

Makes about 1-1/2 quarts

   2 cups milk
   2 cups whipping cream
   1 cup sugar
   1/2 cup packed whole anise or Thai basil leaves
   6 extra-large egg yolks
   2 ounces unsweetened chocolate, broken into pieces
   6 ounces good quality, semisweet chocolate,
      broken into pieces

Combine the milk with 1 cup of the whipping cream, sugar, and basil in a 2-quart, heavy-bottomed nonreactive saucepan. Bruise the leaves against the side of the pan with a wooden spoon. Bring the contents of the pan to a simmer remove from heat. Cover, and let the herbs steep in the liquid for 30 minutes.

Strain the infused cream through a large sieve, pressing on the herb leaves to extract their essence. Return the warm infused cream to the pan, reserving about 1 cup. Lightly whisk the eggs in a small bowl and add about half of the reserved cup of the warm cream to the eggs and whisk, add the remaining cream and whisk again.

129

Whisk the egg and cream mixture into the saucepan and gently reheat the infused cream over low heat. Cook, stirring constantly, until the custard lightly coats a metal spoon, about 5 minutes. Remove from heat.

Melt the chocolate. Whisk about 1/2 of the melted chocolate into the custard. Add the rest of the chocolate to the custard in 3 parts. Adding the chocolate gradually to the custard will keep it from getting grainy.

Strain the cream mixture into a bowl, cool to room temperature, and chill (an ice bath will speed this step). Stir in the remaining 1 cup whipping cream. Freeze according to manufacturer's instructions.

Of course, the ice cream is best served the day it is made, however it keeps well in the freezer for up to 2 weeks. For best flavor, do not serve the ice cream rock hard; allow it to stand at room temperature for 5 to 10 minutes so it softens slightly.

peppermint ice cream
with mini chocolate chips

Use peppermint or spearmint to make this ice cream; peppermint is stronger and spearmint is milder and sweeter; you will need to use a few extra sprigs of spearmint. If you can't find the mini morsels, you can finely chop your own semisweet chocolate in a food processor or with a knife.

Makes a generous quart

2 cups whipping cream
1 cup milk
10 sprigs peppermint
7/8 cup sugar
3 extra-large egg yolks
3/4 cup semisweet mini morsels

In a heavy-bottomed nonreactive pan, combine the cream and milk. Add the mint sprigs and sugar and stir well. Place the pan over medium heat and stir occasionally, until very hot, but not simmering. Remove the pan from the heat, cover and let stand for at least 1/2 hour, or overnight.

Remove the herb sprigs and squeeze them to remove all of their essence; gently reheat the cream to hot, but not simmering. Lightly beat the egg yolks in a small bowl. Add about 1/2 cup of the hot cream mixture to the yolks and whisk well. Return the cream and egg mixture to the pan and whisk well. Cook over low to medium heat, stirring constantly, until it coats a spoon lightly.

Pour the custard through a strainer into a bowl, pressing the leaves to extract their flavor. Let the custard cool a bit and then refrigerate until thoroughly chilled.

Transfer the chilled custard into the container of an ice cream maker and freeze according to the manufacturer's instructions. About halfway through freezing time, add the chocolate mini morsels.

Store the finished ice cream in the freezer until ready to serve; garnish with fresh mint sprigs.

cantaloupe sorbet
with summer herbs

This sorbet makes a refreshing summertime dessert, no matter what herb you choose to add to it. When made with lemon balm or verbena, it has a hint of lemon and seems slightly sweeter; pineapple sage imparts a more subtle herby flavor; and it surprises the palate with spiciness when made with cinnamon or lemon basil. Asti Spumante is sweeter, and champagne is dry and tart, use the larger amount of sugar if you are using champagne.

Serves 8 to 10

> **1/3 to 1/2 cup sugar**
> **1 cup boiling water**
> **10 to 12 lemon balm, pineapple sage, or basil sprigs**
> **1 medium cantaloupe**
> **4 tablespoons packed chervil**
> **1 cup chilled Asti Spumante or champagne**
> **Lemon balm, pineapple sage, or basil leaves for garnish**

In a small saucepan, dissolve the sugar in the water, add the herb leaves, cover, and let the syrup cool.

Remove the seeds from the melon and cut the pulp into chunks; there should be 3-1/2 to 4 cups. Remove the herb leaves from the syrup.

In a food processor or blender, puree the melon with the syrup in batches until smooth. Pour the melon puree into the canister of an ice cream maker, and then stir in the Asti or champagne. Freeze the sorbet according to manufacturer's instructions. Serve garnished with herb leaves or flowers.

citrus sorbet with opal basil

Refreshing on a hot summer day, this sorbet is an eye opener in the dead of winter. I dry opal basil to use for just these purposes, especially since my friend Carolyn ships me a box of Lisbon lemons from the tree in her backyard in California, every January. I can't begin to tell you how wonderfully aromatic, sweet, tart, and fruity these bright yellow orbs are! Suffice it to say, I salivate all the way to the post office and back. If you don't have exotic Lisbon or Meyer, regular lemons and ruby-red grapefruit will do the trick. The prepared liquid is a bright rosy pink with yellow curls of zest before it is frozen, and when it is ready it is a fluffy, slushy medium-pink. First taste is a surprising burst of flavor, followed by tart and sweet, with a blush of lingering perfume.

Makes 1 quart

> **3 cups water**
> **1/2 cup packed fresh opal basil leaves or 3 tablespoons dried opal basil leaves**
> **1 cup sugar**
> **2 large lemons**
> **1 small red or pink grapefruit**
> **Zest of 1 lemon; generous tablespoon**

Bring 2 cups water and the basil leaves to a boil in a nonreactive saucepan. Boil 1 minute and add the sugar. Reduce heat and simmer over low heat for about 4 minutes, until the sugar is dissolved and the liquid is turning purple. Remove from heat and let cool to room temperature.

Meanwhile, remove the zest from 1 of the lemons. Squeeze the lemons and strain the juice, pressing on the pulp to extract as much as possible. Squeeze the grapefruit and repeat the straining process. Stir the zest and juices together; it should measure 1-1/4 cups.

Strain the basil and sugar syrup to remove the basil and add the remaining cup of water. Combine the basil syrup with the fruit juice. If the mixture is chilled first, it will freeze faster.

Freeze the mixture according to the manufacturer's instructions for your ice cream maker. Serve the sorbet when it is ready in sherbet glasses or pretty bowls. If you place the sorbet in the freezer and it becomes hard, allow it to stand at room temperature for 10 or 15 minutes before scooping and serving.

citrus sorbet with opal basil

pineapple sorbet
with pineapple sage blossoms

This refreshing sorbet has intense scarlet flecks of pineapple sage blossoms, which add a visual accent and lend a subtle flavor. If you don't have pineapple sage blooms (*Salvia elegans*), red monarda flowers, would be pretty, but impart a different tea-like taste.

Makes about 1-1/2 quarts

1/2 cup sugar
1 cup boiling water
About 1/4 cup pineapple sage blossoms
1 large, ripe pineapple
Pineapple sage blossoms and leaves for garnish

Dissolve the sugar in the boiling water and set aside to cool. Stir the pineapple sage blossoms into the sugar syrup when it has cooled.

Clean and core the pineapple and cut it into chunks. There should be about 5 cups. In a processor or in the blender in batches, puree the pineapple. Stir the syrup into the puree and blend well.

Pour the pineapple mixture into the container of an ice cream machine and process according to manufacturer's directions. Serve immediately or place in freezer.

If frozen hard, about 10 minutes before serving, allow to sit at room temperature for a few minutes. Blend or process the sorbet to a smooth consistency. Transfer to chilled serving glasses and serve or place in freezer for 5 to 10 minutes.

vanilla & scented geranium sugars

miscellaneous

crystallized edible flowers & herb leaves

vanilla and herb-scented sugar

homemade vanilla bean extract

basic herb syrup

herbs & flowers for making syrups

mocha chocolata cordial

crystallized edible flowers & herb leaves

Good candidates for candying are apple or plum blossoms, borage flowers, lilac florets, rose petals, scented geraniums, and the violas—violets, johnny jump-ups, and pansy petals. When candying leaves, use small, thin ones—I like lemon balm, mint, and anise hyssop leaves. This job takes a little patience; it seems to go more quickly if you do it with a friend. The following recipe will coat quite a few flowers (if you need more, mix up a second batch). If you are concerned about using a raw egg white, powdered pasteurized egg whites are available in the grocery and they work just fine.

Rinsed and dried flower blossoms, separated from the stem, or herb leaves
1 extra large egg white, at room temperature
Few drops of water
About 1 cup superfine sugar

You will need to have a small paint brush or two, wax paper and a baking rack. Spread the wax paper on the baking rack.

In a small bowl combine the egg white with the water and beat lightly with a fork or small whisk until the white just shows a few bubbles. Put the sugar in a shallow dish.

Holding a leaf, flower, or petal in one hand, dip a paint brush into the egg white and gently paint it. Cover the leaf or flower completely, but not excessively. Hold the leaf or flower over the sugar dish and gently sprinkle sugar evenly all over on both sides. Place the leaf or flower on the wax paper to dry. Continue with the rest of the leaves and flowers.

Let the leaves and flowers dry completely, they should be free of moisture. This could take 12 to 36 hours depending on atmospheric humidity. To hasten drying the candied flowers can be placed in an oven overnight with a pilot light, or in a very low oven (about 150 to 200°F) with the door ajar for a few hours.

Store the dried, candied flowers in airtight containers until ready to use. They can be kept for up to 1 year.

vanilla and herb-scented sugar

Scented sugars can easily be made the same way that the Europeans have been making vanilla sugar for years. Placing a vanilla bean, or a handful of herb leaves &/or flowers, in a pint jar of sugar transforms the sugar into a pleasing, fragrant addition to cakes, cookies, custards, whipping cream, and all sorts of sweets. If you do a lot of baking, make this in larger quantities—a quart or half-gallon jar—you will find that you use it often.

Some favorite herbs for making scented sugars are: lemon balm, lemon verbena, orange or peppermint, and scented geraniums. Edible flower choices are lavender, lilac, rose, violets, and anise hyssop.

About 2 cups sugar

> **1 vanilla bean, cut into 3 or 4 pieces or 1 handful of herb leaves &/or flowers**

To prepare scented sugar, use a clean pint jar with a tight-fitting lid. Fill the jar about one-third full with sugar, place 1 or 2 pieces of vanilla bean or a few herb leaves &/or flowers in the sugar. Cover with sugar so that the jar is two-thirds full, add another piece or two of vanilla, or a few more herbs and cover with sugar to fill the jar, leaving about 1/2 inch headspace. Shake the jar and place in a cool, dark place.

The sugar will be ready to use in two to three weeks and will become more flavorful with age. As the sugar is consumed, add more plain sugar to take its place and it will take on the fragrance in the jar.

Since vanilla beans and herbs contain moisture, the sugar will absorb some of it and perhaps cake together, or even harden. If this happens, just use firm pressure to crumble it with your hands, or the back of a wooden spoon.

homemade vanilla bean extract

Most pure vanilla extract is about 35% alcohol, and contains water, sugar, and vanilla bean extractives. It is pretty easy to make your own version. It won't taste just like the commercial brands—it probably won't be quite as intense in vanilla flavor, but I find it very satisfactory. Vodka will allow the most vanilla bean flavor to come through. I often make mine with brandy or rum because I like their flavor. You only use 1 to 2 teaspoons in a recipe, so a little goes a long way. Try experimenting to see what you like best.

Makes about 1 cup or an 8 ounce-bottle, or halve the recipe for a smaller amount

   2 or 3 vanilla beans
   8 ounces of vodka, rum, or brandy

Cut the vanilla beans in half crosswise. Put them into a clean, dark glass, 8-ounce bottle (save used vanilla extract bottles for this). Using a funnel, pour the alcohol into the bottle. Cap the bottle and shake for a minute or two. Label and date the bottle. Place in a cool place out of direct light.

Shake the extract once a day, at least for the first week. I do it whenever I go into the pantry and think about it. I usually uncap it and take a whiff; it is a form of kitchen aromatherapy. You can use it after a week; it is best after 3 or 4 weeks.

The longer it sits, the more intense the flavor. While commercial vanilla extract has the beans removed, I leave the beans in the bottle and as I use the extract, I top it off with more alcohol.

herb syrups

Herb syrups are wonderful flavor essences that are good on all kinds of fruits and used in beverages. Most important, they allow you to add herbal flavor without green specks—not that specks aren't agreeable in some foods—sometimes we just don't want them. For instance, the little bits of texture aren't desirable in a whipping cream or a melt-in-your-mouth chocolate truffle.

With syrups, you can enjoy the health benefits of herbs while using them to sweeten tea and to make natural sodas. They can be added in place of the liquid in cakes, pie filling, and sorbet. Brush the syrups on pound cakes, cupcakes, muffins, or breads just out of the oven. Make these when you have fresh herbs in abundance, their flavor and aroma will bring brightness to fruits, fruit salad, and desserts.

Although I have been making rose, violet, mint, ginger, and vanilla syrups for years, the inspiration for expanding my herbal horizon of syrups came from *The Herb Farm Cookbook* by Jerry Traunfeld, Scribner, 2000. He has many wonderful recipes using herbs syrups, cream, and milk infusions, which capture the herbal essence.

I do play around with the amount of sugar in this recipe—this recipe makes a sweet syrup—depending upon what I am using the syrup for—I often cut the sugar back to 3/4 or 1 cup. For instance, when I make ginger syrup for ginger ale, or a punch that has already sweet ingredients like pineapple juice, I use the lesser amount of sugar. Syrups can also be sweetened with maple syrup or honey, however their flavor will be dominate and lessen the flavor of the herbs.

basic herb syrup

Makes about 2 cups

1-1/2 cups water
1-1/2 cups sugar
About 8 to 10 herb sprigs or a large handful of leaves

To make an herb syrup, combine the water and sugar in a small saucepan, place over moderate heat and bring to a boil, stirring occasionally. Remove from heat, add the herbs bruising the leaves against the side of the pan with a spoon. Cover, remove and let stand for at least 30 minutes and up to overnight.

Remove the leaves and squeeze them into the syrup to extract their flavor. Pour into a clean bottle or jar and label. This syrup can be made ahead and kept in the refrigerator for about 4 weeks.

If you want to keep the syrups for a long period of time, pour them into jars or bottles leaving at least a few inches of headspace, place on the lid or cap, and label. They keep well, frozen, for up to one year. Remove from the freezer the night before using and allow to thaw, or, place the bottle in a bowl of warm (not hot) water to thaw more quickly.

herbs & flowers for making syrups

Amounts of herbs and herb flowers used will vary and depend on the flavor of each individual herb; the list below is for sprigs about 4 or 5 inches long. Use only herbs and flowers that are organically grown and not sprayed with pesticides. Be creative and try your favorite herb, or perhaps a combination.

anise hyssop—6 to 8 sprigs with flowers, or a handful of flowers

basil—6 to 8 sprigs of anise, cinnamon, green, or lemon basil

bay—10 to 12 fresh leaves

ginger—about 1/4 to 1/3 cup thin slices of the root

lavender—10 flower spikes or 1 tablespoon flowers

lemon balm, lemon thyme, or lemon verbena—
    8 to10 sprigs

monarda—10 or 12 leaves, especially the petals of 2 or 3
    blooms

mint—10 to 12 sprigs of orange mint, peppermint, or
    spearmint

rose petals—a generous handful, be sure to taste them for
    flavor first, since they vary enormously!

rosemary—5 or 6 sprigs

sage—4 common sage sprigs; 6 fruit-scented or pineapple
    sage sprigs, especially the flowers

scented geraniums—12 to 15 leaves rose, nutmeg,
    lemon, coconut, apple, ginger, etc., flowers too

tarragon or mexican tarragon—6 to 8 sprigs

vanilla—1 to 2 beans, halved and split lengthwise

herb seeds—about 1 tablespoon bruised anise, coriander, or
    fennel seeds (slightly green are best)

mocha chocolata cordial

This assertive liqueur is for those who love the flavor of mocha—a combination of coffee and chocolate. Five of the six ingredients in this cordial are considered aphrodisiacs—yaya! While this is delicious served in small cordial glasses for sipping, it is also good to use in other preparations. It elevates a cup of hot cocoa to an adult level, makes a great addition to an after dinner coffee drink served with whipped cream, and is quite lovely drizzled over ice cream or pound cake. Combined with eggnog and vanilla ice cream in the blender, served in a martini glass with a dash of nutmeg, it becomes a frosty cocktail that is a cross between traditional holiday eggnog and a Brandy Alexander!

The coffee flavor dominates this cordial, so you can cut the beans back to 1/8 cup if you want equal chocolate flavor. Also, if coffee keeps you (or your guests) awake at night—make this with decaffeinated beans—it is still very stimulating (and no one will know). I use a good quality brandy, but you could use a dark rum. You can use sugar in place of the honey, but then you lose one of your aphrodisiacs. Taste for sweetness and add another 1/4 cup honey if desired.

Makes about 2 cups

　　1/4 cup coffee beans, ground
　　2 cups brandy (about 80 proof)
　　1 cup honey
　　6 tablespoons unsweetened cocoa
　　1 whole vanilla bean, cut in half lengthwise, and then
　　　crosswise
　　1/2 teaspoon freshly grated nutmeg

Combine the coffee beans with the brandy and let stand for an hour. Strain the brandy through dampened cheesecloth to remove the coffee grounds. Pour the brandy into a clean bottle or jar. Add the honey, cocoa, vanilla bean, and nutmeg. Put the lid on the bottle and shake well.

Shake once or twice a day for a week. Strain off the vanilla beans if desired, or leave them. Pour into a nice bottle, label, and keep in a cool dark place.

bibliography

Baggett, Nancy. *The International Chocolate Cookbook.* New York: Stewart, Taboori, and Chang, 1991.

Belsinger, Susan. *Flowers in the Kitchen.* Loveland, CO: Interweave Press, 1991.
_____. *Herb Companion.* Topeka, KS: Ogden Publications, 2004-2005.
_____. *Natural Home.* Loveland, CO: Interweave Press, 2004-2005.

DeBaggio, Thomas, and Belsinger, Susan. *Basil: An Herb Lover's Guide.* Loveland, CO: Interweave Press, 1996.

Dille, Carolyn, and Belsinger, Susan. *Herbs in the Kitchen.* Loveland, CO: Interweave Press, 1992.

Medrich, Alice. *Bittersweet.* New York: Artisan, 2003.

Shere, Lindsey Remolif. *Chez Panisse Desserts.* New York: Random House, 1985.

Traunfeld, Jerry. *The Herbfarm Cookbook.* New York: Scribner, 2000.

Yockelson, Lisa. *Baking by Flavor.* New York: Wiley and Sons, Inc., 2002.

_____*A Country Baking Treasury.* New York: Harper Collins Publishers, 1988.

index

numbers in boldface are photographs

150

151